SCOTTISH
WILD FLOWERS

SCOTTISH
WILD FLOWERS

Mary McMurtrie

GARDEN • ART • PRESS

To
Professor Ian Alexander

First published 2001
©2001 Mary McMurtrie
World copyright reserved

ISBN 1 870673 38 7

British Library Cataloguing-in-Publication Data
A catalogue record for this book is available from the British Library

Printed in England on Consort Royal Era Satin paper from the
Donside Paper Company, Aberdeen, by
Garden Art Press, Woodbridge, Suffolk IP12 1DS

PLATE 1

Frontispiece - Some Rare Scottish Native Plants

1 Blue Sow-thistle *Cicerbita alpina* **Compositae**
The tall stem ends in a pale lilac-blue inflorescence (raceme). The lower leaves are lyre-shaped with a large end lobe.

On wet mountain rocks. July – September.

2 Blue Heath *Phyllodoce caerulea* **Ericaceae**
Oval, purple, five-lobed, drooping flowers with long stalks. Leaves are linear and green on both sides.

Rocky moors in Central Scotland. June – July.

3 Diapensia *Diapensia lapponica* **Diapensiaceae**
A cushion-forming, evergreen, dwarf shrub, with oval leathery leaves in dense rosettes. Solitary white five-lobed flowers.

An Arctic plant only known on two sites. May – June.

4 Drooping Saxifrage *Saxifraga cernua* **Saxifragaceae**
Resembles the Meadow Saxifrage but the stem is shorter. There are red bulbils in the axils of the upper leaves. Lower leaves are kidney-shaped and in a rosette. The flowers are white and solitary.

Mountain rocks (calcareous). July.

5 Alpine Forget-me-not *Myosotis alpestris* **Boraginaceae**
Low-growing, with blue flowers and long-stalked lower leaves.

On basic mountain rocks. July – September.

6 Rock Whitlow Grass *Draba norvegica* **Cruciferae**
Small and tufted, with basal rosettes of pointed linear leaves, and short leafless flower stems with heads of tiny white flowers.

On high mountain tops. July – August.

7 Red Alpine Catchfly *Lychnis alpina* **Caryophyllaceae**
Rose flowers in rounded heads on short glabrous stems. Linear, sharply-pointed leaves on the stems and in dense rosettes at the base.

Mountains in Angus. June – July.

8 Alpine Fleabane *Erigeron borealis* **Compositae**
The short hairy stem usually bears a solitary flower head, with purple ray florets. The hairy leaves clasp the stem and are also in a basal rosette.

Mountain rock ledges. July – August.

9 Tufted Saxifrage *Saxifraga cespitosa* **Saxifragaceae**
Dense cushions with leaves in compact rosettes. Flowers are white, on short stalks.

High mountain rocks. May –July.

10 Arctic Sandwort *Arenaria norvegica* **Caryophyllaceae**
A compact tuft, with stems branching close to the base. The crowded leaves are small, oval, and fleshy, the flowers white.

Rocky places. West Sutherland, Shetland and Rhum. June – July.

11 Snow Gentian, Alpine Gentian *Gentiana nivalis* **Gentianaceae**
An erect, slender annual.

Rock ledges on mountains in Perth and Angus. July – September.

Acknowledgements

I should like to acknowledge the many kind friends who have given so much time and effort in helping me to prepare this book, especially Professor Ian Alexander for the hours spent editing, checking all the plant descriptions and patiently correcting my mistakes. I am most grateful to the following:

Nature Conservancy Council, North East (Scotland) Region.
 St. Cyrus Nature Reserve, Mr. D. Carstairs, Warden.
 Sands of Forvie and Ythan Estuary, Mr. R. Davis, Warden.
 Muir of Dinnet, Mr. Parkin, Warden.
University of Aberdeen Botany Department.
 Professor Ian Alexander, F.R.S.E., B.Sc., Ph.D., F.R.S.E.
 Dr. C. C. Wilcock, B.Sc., M.Sc., Ph.D., F.L.S., Lecturer in Botany.
 Mr. R. Rutherford, Cruickshank Botanic Garden, Aberdeen.

Mr. J. Beverley, Miss E. R. Bullard, M.B.E., Mr. John Coutts, Mrs. Dalzel-Job, Mrs. E. Dickenson, Mr. A. B. Duguid, A.H.R.H.S., S.H.M., Mr. J. Fraser, Pinewood Park Nurseries, Aberdeen, Mrs. Jean Gardner, Mrs. M. I. C. Harbord, Mr. Douglas Haston, Mrs. Elspeth Haston, Ms. Elspeth M. Haston, M.Sc., Mrs. B. Hone, Mrs. Ann Howlett, Mrs. Iain Mathieson, Misses E. and I. Moffatt, Mr R. W. Rutherford, The University of Reading, Mr. and Mrs. M. Stone, Sir George Taylor, D.Sc., F.R.S., L.L.D., F.R.S.E., F.L.S., V.M.H., Miss Mary McCallum Webster, Mr. Douglas P. Willis, M.A., M.Litt., F.S.A. Scot., Mrs. D. Willis, Mrs. Woolcombe, Dr. J. R. Young, B.Sc., Dr. and Mrs. Mark Young, Mrs H. J. Younger.

And for loan of books:-
Mrs. E. Birse, Dr. Andrew Gardner, B.Sc., Ph.D., North East of Scotland Library, Dr. Alan J. Silverside, Paisley College of Technology, Mrs. F. B. Watson.

Contents

Preface

In Professor Alexander's words, this book '…is intended to delight and inform the reader and to promote an interest in our native flora by presenting it in an attractive (aesthetically pleasing) way.'

In Scotland we have a varied and interesting flora. Many unspoilt areas remain such as parts of the Highlands, the mountains and moors of Central Scotland, the islands of the West and the long and varied coastline. Nature reserves under the Nature Conservancy Council protect the many rare plants as well as those that were once common but are now becoming scarce.

As an aid to identification, the plants in this book have been arranged, as far as possible, in colour groups. There are always variations, however, and many flowers change colour as they age. The descriptions face the illustrations and include the common name, botanical name, plant family, the habit and time of flowering. Whenever possible, the plants of the same family are kept together within the particular colour section. They were drawn to their actual size, possibly slightly reduced for reproduction.

The scientific names used here are those given in the second edition of the *Flora of the British Isles* by A.R. Clapham, T.G. Tutin, and E.F. Warburg. These have been revised after the *New Flora of the British Isles* (1997) by Clive A. Stace. Traditional and familiar family names have been kept. Revision would give the following equivalents:

Compositae – Asteraceae; Cruciferae – Brassicaceae; Hydrocotylaceae – Apiaceae; Hypericaceae – Clusiaceae; Labiatae – Lamiaceae; Lobeliaceae – Campanulaceae; Parnassiaceae – Saxifragaceae; Umbelliferae – Apiaceae; Trilliaceae – Liliaceae.

Foreword

Many years ago I was fortunate to be introduced to Mary McMurtrie, and to spend happy hours with her in the wonderful garden which she created at Balbithan. My lasting memory of those times is of Mary sitting at her easel by the window in the quiet of the library at Balbithan, with specimens from the Scottish flora ranged in jars and pots along the windowsill, faithfully recording them for a publishing project on Scottish Wild Flowers. Her love of flowers and her enthusiasm for the project were palpable, as she painted and talked infectiously about the treasures soon to be delivered by one of her collectors. For many years I feared that these wonderful paintings would never reach a wider public, and I am delighted that this will now be possible.

What is it that makes Mary McMurtrie's flower paintings so special? For me it is how her soft and delicate watercolours catch the essence of the plant, and how she brings it to life in the easy and natural way she positions it on the paper. The eye of the artist conveys something that the lens of the camera can never achieve.

These days someone seeking ways to identify wild flowers is spoilt for choice, for there are a plethora of accurately illustrated handbooks – not to mention all the information accessible via the Internet. Those sources may educate and inform – but they will not delight, and reward your aesthetic sense, in the way that this book will. Mary's paintings will inspire you to look afresh at our beautiful native flora, to become more knowledgeable about it and to marvel, as she so clearly does, at the beauty and diversity of plants.

Professor Ian Alexander
Regius Professor of Botany
University of Aberdeen

Glossary

Achene – small one-seeded nutlet formed from a single carpel.

Axil – the upper angle between a leaf and stem.

Base-rich – soils containing relatively large amounts of free basic ions, e.g. calcium, magnesium, etc.

Berry – fleshy fruit containing one or more seeds.

Biennial – plant that lives for two seasons, flowering and fruiting in the second.

Bract – a small leaf intermediate between calyx and normal leaves, often close below flower.

Bulbil – small bulb usually above ground in leaf axil, or on a leaf edge, which can fall off and form a new plant.

Calyx – the ring of sepals surrounding the petals.

Capsule – a dry fruit that splits open to release seeds.

Carpel – a division of the ovary of seed vessel.

Corolla – petals of a flower, used collectively.

Corymb – flat-topped flower cluster where outer flower stalks are longest.

Cyme – inflorescence where the terminal flower opens first.

Dioecious – having male and female flowers on different plants.

Disc-floret – the inner tubular floret such as in a daisy, the ray floret is the outer, often strap-shaped floret.

Dune-slacks – the hollows, often damp or wet, between dunes.

Floret – individual small flower, especially in the flower-head of the Daisy family.

Inflorescence – a grouping of flowers on a stem.

Involucre – a ring of bracts at base of flower-head.

Leaflets – the separate leaf-blades of a compound leaf such as clover or vetch.

Node – the point on a stem where a leaf or whorl of leaves is attached.

Obovate leaf – has the widest part towards the tip.

Pappus – the hairs on top of some fruits such as dandelion.

Perianth – collective term for calyx and corolla of a flower.

Petals – the inner flower leaves that surround stamens, etc.

Pinnate – compound leaf with (usually) opposite pairs of leaflets such as vetch.

Pinnatifid – deeply cut into lobes which do not meet the midrib but are connected.

Pollinium – a sticky mass of pollen grains, usually in orchids, which adheres to insects' heads and can be carried to another flower.

Raceme – a long inflorescence where the lowest flower opens first, others in sequence, and the flowers are stalked.

Rhizome – a creeping underground stem, often fleshy.

Scarious – thin and dry, not green, e.g. tip of bract in Fleabane.

Sepal – one of the outer ring of floral leaves (calyx), usually green, surrounding the peta

Sessile – stalkless.

Spike – an unbranched raceme without stalks to individual flowers.

Spur – the hollow tube from the back of a flower which usually contains nectar (orchid).

Stamen – the male or pollen-bearing part of a flower.

Stigma – the pollen-receiving (usually sticky) tip of the style.

Stipule – a leaf-like or scale-like appendage at the base of a leaf-stalk; there is often a pair.

Stolon – a runner, not necessarily forming a new plant at its tip.

Style – the stalk-like part that connects the stigma (or stigmas) at the tip of a carpel or several joined carpels, with the rest of the ovary.

Trifoliate leaf – a compound leaf with three leaflets only, as Clover.

Tuber – a swollen part of the root or underground stem, which stores food.

Umbel – a flat-topped inflorescence where the branches all arise from one point at the top of the main stem, a simple umbel is composed of one whorl, in a compound umbel each branch has a secondary umbel.

Winged stem – a stem with one or more flanges along its length.

PLATE 2

1   White Butterbur   *Petasites albus*   **Compositae**

The flowers are closely bunched together in small clusters in a spike at the end of the stem which is covered with leafy bracts. The flower-stems rise 15–30cm from thick reddish rhizomes and appear first, followed by the leaves which are heart-shaped and toothed, downy and white beneath, on long stalks direct from the root. These ultimately grow very large, up to about 90cm across. The White Butterbur is an introduced plant, locally common especially in Aberdeenshire and Northern Scotland; the native plant *P. hybridus* is pink, and is common in the south.

Damp places, roadsides, edges of woods. April — May.

2   Wood Sorrel   *Oxalis acetosella*   **Oxalidaceae**

The white flowers are solitary, frail and delicate, lightly veined with mauve. Like the leaves they rise directly from the reddish creeping rhizomes which form a matted growth in the leafy humus. Their slender stems have a pair of bractioles about half-way up. The leaves are smooth and light green, resembling clover leaves, with the leaflets often tightly folded back against each other. They are sometimes purplish on the undersides.

Woods and shady hedge banks, mountains. April — May.

3   Wood Anemone, Wind Flower   *Anemone nemorosa*   **Ranunculaceae**

The solitary flowers, delicately beautiful, are white, often tinted with pink or mauve, especially on the undersides. Six or more petal-like sepals form the star-like flower, with numerous stamens in the centre. About two-thirds up the flower-stalk there is a whorl of three leaves, stalked, with deeply cut lobes, almost ferny in appearance. The basal leaves are similar, and rise at intervals from the creeping rhizome.

It carpets the ground in deciduous woods and shady banks. March — May.

1.

2 -

3 -

PLATE 3

1   Marsh Stitchwort   *Stellaria palustris*   Caryophyllaceae
The flowers resemble those of the Greater Stitchwort but are smaller. The stems are slender, weak and brittle, with both flowering and non-flowering shoots; the former are branching with several long-stalked flowers at the head. The bracts have broad, smooth chaffy margins and a narrow green central strip. The leaves, usually glaucous, are very narrowly lanceolate and without stalks.

Marshes and fens, local, mostly in the south. May — July.

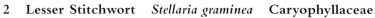

2   Lesser Stitchwort   *Stellaria graminea*   Caryophyllaceae
This is much smaller, more delicate in leaf and stem, and even more straggling in habit. The tiny starry flowers, with sepals equal to the petals in length, grow on widely branching stems and have thread-like stalks; the bracts are scarious (thin, brownish and dry) with hairy margins. The smooth, lance-shaped unstalked leaves are in pairs along the stems.

Common, growing on roadside banks and in grassy ditches. May — August.

3   Greater Stitchwort   *Stellaria holostea*   Caryophyllaceae
The five shining white petals are split half-way down and are longer than the sepals; the bracts are leaf-like. The flowers are in clusters at the ends of the slender straggling stems, each on a thread-like stalk. The stems are square in section and have pairs of slightly glaucous unstalked leaves at intervals, lance-shaped, tapering from a wide base to a long fine point and rough on the margins. The plants form a twisted mass, partly prostrate and partly climbing through the undergrowth.

Hedgerows, grassy roadside banks and ditches. March — June.

4   Chickweed   *Stellaria media*   Caryophyllaceae
This is a very common annual weed of gardens and cultivated ground. The long, branching, creeping and ascending shoots have opposite, light green leaves which are broadly oval, stalkless or almost so. The numerous flowers, very tiny, are long-stalked, with deeply cleft petals not exceeding the sepals. The fruit stalks curve downward.

All the year.

1.

2.

3.

4.

P<small>LATE</small> 4

1   Common Mouse-ear Chickweed   *Cerastium fontanum*   Caryophyllaceae
A perennial, occasionally annual, low, densely hairy plant with a slender creeping stock from which rise decumbent non-flowering shoots and erect flowering shoots. The flowers are white with deeply-cleft petals equal to, or a little longer than, the sepals. They are in loose clusters. The fruit is a slightly curved cylindrical capsule about twice as long as the calyx.

A very common plant of waysides, waste places and cultivated ground. March — October.

2   Sticky Mouse-ear Chickweed   *Cerastium glomeratum*   Caryophyllaceae
A glandular-hairy annual with erect or ascending flowering shoots with flowers in dense terminal heads. These flowers are white with cleft petals about the same length as the narrow pointed sepals, and the cylindrical capsule is curved. The leaves are yellowish-green and broadly oval.

Also a common weed of arable land and waste places. March — October.

3   Alpine Mouse-ear Chickweed   *Cerastium alpinum*   Caryophyllaceae
Prostrate and mat-forming, with ascending flowering shoots. The large white flowers have petals twice as long as the sepals and are not very deeply cleft. The stems and oval leaves are densely covered with long, soft, white hairs, so that the whole plant has a very silvery appearance. On mountain rock-ledges, especially on granite and schists.

Local on high mountains. June — August.

PLATE 5

1   Corn Spurrey   *Spergula arvensis*   Caryophyllaceae
An annual with long, weak, prostrate or ascending stems, sticky and hairy with clustered, narrow, grass-like leaves which are furrowed below and have tiny stipules that soon fall. The stems are much branched and forking, with white flowers whose sepals have a narrow chaffy-edged (scarious) margin and are about as long as the petals. The flowers are long-stalked, and when in fruit their stalks characteristically hang down.

Common in sandy arable land. June — October.

2   Spring Sandwort   *Minuartia verna*   Caryophyllaceae
A small tufted perennial, mat-forming, with erect flowering and non-flowering shoots. The leaves are very narrow and grass-like, and are three-veined, in tufts along the stems. The flowers are white and starry, with narrow, scarious sepals. The petals are longer than the sepals and the distinctive anthers are bright red.

Dry rocks and screes. May — September.

3   Knotted Pearlwort   *Sagina nodosa*   Caryophyllaceae
A low tufted perennial, with curving thread-like stems which have knots or clusters of narrow, pointed leaves, largest at the base. The flowers are few and small, with five, pointed, un-notched petals twice the length of the sepals, ten stamens, and five styles.

Bare, damp, sandy or peaty ground on dunes or heaths. July — September.

4   Mossy Cyphel   *Minuartia sedoides* (syn. *Cherleria sedoides*)   Caryophyllaceae
A yellow-green mossy cushion plant, with densely tufted leafy shoots. The non-flowering shoots are more prostrate, and the flowering shoots are erect, all rising from a branching woody stock with a very long tap-root. The tiny solitary flowers are usually without petals, though sometimes present in the male flowers.

On rocky slopes of mountains to over 3,000ft, and on shingle at sea level near Montrose. June — August.

1.

2.

3.

4.

P<small>LATE</small> 6

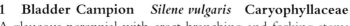

1   Bladder Campion   *Silene vulgaris*   Caryophyllaceae
A glaucous perennial with erect branching and forking stems carrying clusters of white flowers. The petals are rather narrow and are deeply cleft with small inconspicuous scales or bosses at the base of each petal. Styles three, with stamens (hermaphrodite). The calyx is large, inflated and bladder-shaped, mauvish and strongly veined, narrowing at the mouth, with six erect teeth. The leaves at the base have short stalks, the stem leaves are clasping, all are narrowly oval, tapering, smooth and grey-green. The stem is swollen at the nodes.

Common on grassy slopes, roadsides, especially calcareous and sandy soils. June – August.

2   White Campion   *Silene latifolia* ssp. *alba*   Caryophyllaceae
The large white flowers have five deeply notched petals with prominent two-lobed scales at the base. Male and female flowers are on different plants (dioecious); female with five styles, and a rather wider calyx, but on both plants the calyx is ribbed and hairy and has five pointed teeth which remain erect. The upper leaves are in pairs, clasping the stem and are lance-shaped; the lower leaves are large, stalked and taper towards the base. The whole plant is softly hairy.

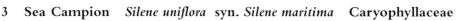

Hedges, waste places and cultivated land. May – September.

3   Sea Campion   *Silene uniflora* syn. *Silene maritima*   Caryophyllaceae
The flower has a rounded appearance, with broader petals which are not so deeply cleft. The flowers are often solitary, they have three styles and stamens, and the calyx is inflated, but not narrowing at the mouth, the six teeth are recurved in the capsule. It is not so tall, and has both ascending flowering shoots, and prostrate non-flowering shoots which form a spreading grey-green cushion.

On cliffs and shingle by the sea, also on mountains. June – August.

PLATE 7

1   Nottingham Catchfly   *Silene nutans*   Caryophyllaceae
A hairy perennial with short non-flowering shoots and flowering shoots which are downy below and sticky above. The basal leaves are spoon-shaped narrowing to a long stalk; the stem leaves are narrow and stalkless; all are softly hairy especially along the margins. The drooping flowers are creamy-white with five narrow, deeply cleft petals that are in-rolled by day, and open and fragrant at night.

Shingle beaches, dry slopes and base-rich rocks and cliffs. Local, east coast north to Kincardineshire. May – July.

2   Sea Sandwort   *Honckenya peploides*   Caryophyllaceae
The leafy flowering and non-flowering shoots rise from long pale slender stolons which creep in sand or shingle. The flowering stems have pairs of stalkless, very fleshy, oval leaves which have translucent wavy margins and downward pointing tips. The small, solitary, greenish-white flowers have obovate petals which equal the blunt fleshy sepals in the male flowers but are shorter in the female. There are ten stamens and usually three styles. The three-lobed capsules, resembling green peas, split open to release the bright chestnut-coloured seeds.

Common on sandy and shingle beaches. May – August.

3   Scottish Asphodel   *Tofieldia pusilla*   Liliaceae
The rigid, three to five-veined, grass-like leaves rise in tufts from a short rhizome, but are mostly at the base. The small, greenish-white flowers are in a close raceme at the end of a slender stem.

Rare, growing by springs and streams on mountains from 700-3,000ft. June – August.

1.

3.

2.

PLATE 8

1   Scentless Mayweed   *Tripleurospermum inodorum*   **syn.** *Matricaria perforata*   **Compositae**
Annual or biennial. This comprises a variable group, all having white 'daisy' flower-heads set singly at the ends of the branching stems, which have lacy, finely-divided leaves at intervals. There are two subspecies: the first is very common on bare ground, roadsides and edges of cultivated ground; the second, *M. perforata* ssp. *maritimum* (Sea Mayweed), is very similar, only the leaf segments are thicker.

July — September.

2   Ox-eye Daisy,   *Leucanthemum vulgare*   **Compositae Marguerite, Gowan**
      syn. *Chrysanthemum leucanthemum*
Perennial. This is the largest of these 'daisies' and is taller and sturdier than the Mayweeds, with strong erect, flowering stems which may be slightly branched. There are a few narrow, stalkless stem leaves and the broad basal leaves, with long stalks, are dark green, contrasting with the brilliant white of the flowers.

Pastures and roadsides. June — September.

3   Daisy   *Bellis perennis*   **Compositae**
Well-known and common everywhere, preferring the short turf of our lawns. The white ray-florets are often tipped with pink, and the solitary flowers on their short stalks rise from rosettes of slightly toothed, spoon-shaped leaves that lie close to the ground. The flowers close at night.

It is in flower practically throughout the year.

1.

2.

3.

PLATE 9

1   Feverfew   *Tanacetum parthenium* **syn.** *Chrysanthemum partheniu*   **Compositae**
A tall, erect, strongly aromatic perennial, with the flowers loosely grouped at the heads of branching stems, technically termed a corymb. Each has a long stalk and short, broad ray-florets. The leaves are yellowish-green, downy and pinnate; the leaflets are also pinnate-lobed, but the upper leaves are less divided.

Probably an introduced plant, but frequent on waste ground and banks. July – August.

2   Sneezewort   *Achillea ptarmica*   **Compositae**
Perennial. The erect stems rise from a creeping woody stock with the flowers again – as above – in a rather loose cluster. The florets are broad and rather square-ended, smaller than those of Feverfew, and the centres are greenish-grey, later becoming yellow. The leaves are long and narrow, with undulating edges and taper to a point. The whole plant has a greyish look, and is covered with white hairs.

Damp meadows, marshes and by streams. July – August.

3   Yarrow   *Achillea millefolium*   **Compositae**
The erect stems, furrowed, greyish-green and sometimes woolly, rise from spreading, far-creeping stolons, with the small flowers, usually white, but occasionally pink, forming flat heads at the branching tops (again a corymb, but closer than the two above). The ray florets are as broad as long, and are three-toothed at the tips. The leaves are finely cut and divided so as to have a feathery appearance, the basal leaves are long and stalked, while those on the stem are shorter, stalkless, and often have two or three small axillary leaves. The plant is strongly scented.

Grassy banks and waysides, pastures. June – August.

1.

2.

3.

PLATE 10

1   Mountain Everlasting, Cats-foot   *Antennaria dioica*   Compositae
A perennial with above-ground, creeping woody stolons which root at the nodes. The unstalked leaves are spathulate, dark green above, white and woolly beneath. They form a basal rosette, and are also along the erect flowering stems. The flower heads are in close clusters at the tips of the stems, male and female on separate plants. The male flowers have bracts which spread like petals. The female bracts are narrow and erect, later crowned by the white pappus of the seeds. Flower colour varies, pink or white.

Heaths, dry mountain slopes. June – July.

2   English Stonecrop   *Sedum anglicum*   Crassulaceae
Evergreen, with mat-forming creeping and rooting stems and erect flowering and non-flowering branches. All are closely set with small, rounded, unstalked, succulent leaves, spirally arranged and usually reddish. The flowers have five narrow white petals, tinged with pink at the back.

Rocks, dunes and shingle on coasts. June – September.

3   Chickweed Wintergreen   *Trientalis europaea*   Primulaceae
The white starry flowers, usually one or two, are on thread-like stalks rising from a whorl of five to six oval pointed leaves at the top of a slender stem. There are a few smaller leaves, alternate and well spaced, further down the stem.

Pine woods and mossy turf on moors. June – July.

4   Round-leaved Sundew   *Drosera rotundifolia*   Droseraceae
A perennial with small rosettes, very common among sphagnum moss and wet places on the hills and moors. The leaves are rounded with short, hairy stalks, and the upper surfaces are covered with bright red glandular hairs which enclose and digest small insects. The white short-stalked flowers are grouped in two rows at the end of a long leafless stem, which rises from the leaf rosette.

June – August.

5   Great Sundew   *Drosera anglica*   Droseraceae
This is a larger plant with longer narrow leaves also covered on the upper surface with bright red glandular hairs, and with similar white flowers. The flower stem rises from the centre of the leaf rosette. It grows in the wetter parts of bogs in the north and west where it makes bright patches of colour.

July – August.

1.

2.

3.

4.

5.

PLATE 11

1   Grass of Parnassus   *Parnassia palustris*   Parnassiaceae

One of our loveliest wild flowers. The five white petals are delicately veined, and as well as the fertile stamens, which are as long as the petals, there are five shorter staminodes, or infertile stamens, which are fan-shaped with yellow glands on the tips. The flowers are solitary on long smooth stems; near the base there is a single, heart-shaped leaf which clasps the stem, and the basal leaves, long-stalked, are also heart-shaped and shiny underneath.

Marshes and moors. July − October.

2   Cloudberry, Aivrons   *Rubus chamaemorus*   Rosaceae

The lovely, solitary, white flowers are conspicuous among their dark green, crinkled leaves, paler beneath, and borne on the stem a little below the flower. The male and female flowers are borne on different plants. When the petals fall the red calyx is very noticeable, and later the large heads of raspberry-like, bright orange, ripe fruits are brilliant.

Damp mountain moors and bogs. June − August.

3   Mountain Avens   *Dryas octopetala*   Rosaceae

The white flowers, with their boss of yellow stamens, characteristically have eight petals, though sometimes more, and are solitary on hairy, reddish stalks rising from the spreading prostrate stems, which branch and intertwine to form a dense, wide, evergreen mat. In fruit the styles persist and form a feathery head. The small dark green leaves are densely white and tomentose beneath, and they, too, have a characteristic shape, like tiny oak-leaves.

Rock ledges and crevices on mountains and down to sea level in the north. Lime-loving. June − July.

1.

2.

3.

PLATE 12

1   Barren Strawberry   *Potentilla sterilis*   Rosaceae
This is perennial and resembles the Wild Strawberry at first glance, but there are various points of difference. This has no red berry, but a dry fruit; the petals of the flowers are widely separated and the flowers are smaller; the leaflets are also smaller and broader with the terminal tooth much smaller than the others, and they are dull bluish-green. The stock is rather woody, ending in a rosette of leaves and frequently sending out prostrate stolons. The spreading hairs on the undersides of the leaflets also serve to distinguish it.

Wood margins, open woods, but not in North Scotland. March — May.

2   Wild Strawberry   *Fragaria vesca*   Rosaceae
Very much smaller in every way than the garden strawberry, but spreading in similar fashion with long arching runners which root at the nodes to form fresh plants. The petals of the small flowers are close, almost overlapping, and the little, red, occasionally white, berries have reflexed sepals. The leaves have three bright green leaflets, pale underneath, deeply grooved, coarsely toothed, and covered with silky adpressed hairs. The leaf-stalks are long and are also hairy; they rise from a rather thick, woody rootstock.

Woodland clearings and shady banks. May — July.

3   Burnet Rose, Scots Rose   *Rosa pimpinellifolia*   Rosaceae
Erect but low-growing, spreading by suckers and forming large, very prickly patches. The reddish stems are thickly covered with prickles and stiff bristles. There are from three to five pairs of small, oval or round blunt, serrated leaflets. The flowers are cream-white, solitary, with narrow sepals, and the rounded fruits become purplish-black.

Dunes, sandy heaths, especially near the sea. North to Caithness and Outer Hebrides, but widespread, both south, and throughout Northern Europe, and north to Siberia. May — July.

1.

2.

3.

PLATE 13

1   Field Rose, Trailing Rose   *Rosa arvensis*   Rosaceae
The stems, with sparse, hooked prickles are very long, and more trailing in habit than any other of our native roses. The flowers are white, in terminal groups of 2–5, and have a faint scent. They have numerous stamens, and the styles are united in a projecting column. The hips are red.

It is more common in the south. June – July.

PLATE 14

1 Meadowsweet *Filipendula ulmaria* **Rosaceae**
The fragrant, creamy-white frothing heads of tiny flowers on the tall leafy stems are a familiar sight along roadside ditches and in swampy ground by banks of streams and wet meadows. The flowers have five petals, five sepals and many prominent stamens. The fruit consists of six to ten carpels tightly twisted together. The large lower leaves are stalked, dark green and deeply ridged, usually downy and white below, with eight or more pairs of oval, pointed, sharp-toothed large leaflets alternating with pairs of tiny ones.

June — August.

2 Mossy Saxifrage *Saxifraga hypnoides* **Saxifragaceae**
Mat-forming and mossy in appearance with flowering rosettes and long sterile, trailing leafy shoots. The rosette leaves are three to five-lobed, pointed; those on the sterile shoots are undivided. The flower stems are erect, with a loose cluster of white, five-petalled flowers.

Rock ledges, screes, on hills and mountains. April — July.

3 Meadow Saxifrage *Saxifraga granulata* **Saxifragaceae**
The five-petalled white flowers are in an open cluster (cyme) at the end of an erect, sticky stem which rises from a rosette of stalked, kidney-shaped, blunt-toothed leaves, often withered by the time of flowering. The upper leaves are few and narrower. Bulbils are produced at the base of the plant, in the axils of the basal leaves.

Dry, sandy grass-land, in the south and west. April — June.

Plate 15

1   Alpine Bistort   *Persicaria vivipara*   **syn.** *Polygonum viviparum*   **Polygonaceae**
A small, slender and erect perennial, with tiny white, sometimes pink, flowers closely grouped at the head of the stem; lower down there are small brownish-red bulbils. The narrow lance-shaped upper leaves clasp the stem, the lower leaves are stalked.

Mountains, grassy places, wet rocks. Sea level in Sutherland. June – August.

2   Northern Rock-cress   *Arabis petraea*   **syn.** *Cardaminopsis petraea*   **Cruciferae**
A small cushion perennial with a tap root, from which shoots with leafy rosettes and erect flowering stems arise, each with a few little, four-petalled, white flowers. The basal leaves are stalked and lobed with a larger end lobe (pinnatifid).

Alpine rocks, to near sea level. June – August.

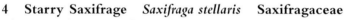

3   Dwarf Cornel   *Cornus suecica*   **Cornaceae**
The tiny, purplish-black flowers, closely grouped, are surrounded by four oval, white, petal-like bracts, sometimes tinged with pink at the tips. They are at the end of short, leafy stems. The leaves are stalkless, oval and pointed, with well-marked veins from the base. The fruit is red, but infrequent.

Moors on mountains, usually under heather or blaeberry. July – August.

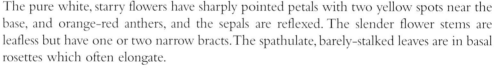

4   Starry Saxifrage   *Saxifraga stellaris*   **Saxifragaceae**
The pure white, starry flowers have sharply pointed petals with two yellow spots near the base, and orange-red anthers, and the sepals are reflexed. The slender flower stems are leafless but have one or two narrow bracts. The spathulate, barely-stalked leaves are in basal rosettes which often elongate.

Mountains, by streams and on wet stony ground. June – August.

5   Heath Bedstraw   *Galium saxatile*   **Rubiaceae**
A mat-forming perennial, the non-flowering shoots are prostrate and the flowering ones are erect. The tiny flowers are in open, few-flowered clusters, they are pure white and four-petalled. The leaves, in whorls of about six to eight, lance-shaped but more rounded on the prostrate stems, have minute forward-pointing prickles on the edges, a distinguishing feature.

Heaths and moors. June – August.

6   Intermediate Wintergreen   *Pyrola media*   **Pyrolaceae**
The blunt rounded leaves, stalked, shiny and dark green, rise from the end of a slender, creeping rhizome. The long, smooth, reddish flower-stem bears at the top several globular flowers, white, faintly tinged with pink, with the style protruding and slightly longer than the stamens.

Woods, moors, commonest in pinewoods. June – August.

[All mountain flowers except *Pyrola media*. The rest of Pyrolaceae follow on the next page.]

1.

2.

3.

4.

5.

6.

PLATE 16

1   One-flowered Wintergreen   *Moneses uniflora*   Pyrolaceae
This perennial is small with large, solitary, drooping, white flowers, which have straight, long styles and five-lobed stigmas. The stamens are in groups of five. The oval, pale green leaves are stalked, and are opposite.

Pinewoods, but very rare. June — August.

2   Serrated Wintergreen   *Orthilia secunda*   Pyrolaceae
The stems are short and the oval, stalked, light green leaves are minutely toothed. The greenish-white flowers are in a dense, nodding, one-sided spike, with a protruding stigma which has five small lobes. The sepals are small and blunt.

Woods, damp rock ledges, local, ascending to 2,400ft. July — August.

3   Common Wintergreen   *Pyrola minor*   Pyrolaceae
The evergreen leaves are in a loose rosette from the creeping rhizome, oval and rather blunt, light green and stalked. The flowers are globular, pinkish-white, with five petals and five tiny sepals. The straight style is shorter than the stamens and ovary, and the stigma has five spreading lobes. The flowers are closely set at the end of the erect stem.

Pinewoods, moors, acid dunes, ascending to 3,750ft. in Perth, but rather local. June — August.

4   Round-leaved Wintergreen   *Pyrola rotundifolia*   Pyrolaceae
The longer-stalked leaves are dark green, shiny and rounded. The flowers, loosely spaced, are white, wide open and almost flat, with a long style which curves down and then up.

Mountain ledges, open woods, fens, dune-slacks, usually calcareous, Scottish Highlands. July — September.

1.

2.

3.

4.

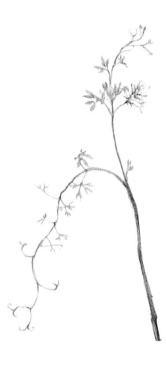

PLATE 17

1   White Climbing Fumitory,   *Ceratocapnos claviculata*   **Fumariaceae**
Climbing Corydalis   **syn.** *Corydalis claviculata*
An annual, climbing, much-branched plant of delicate appearance with red stems and pinnate leaves, small divided leaflets, and the rachis or common stalk ending in a branched tendril. The tiny creamy-white flowers, tinged with green, are in a close raceme at the end of a long stalk which rises from the main stem opposite a leaf-stalk.

Woods and shady rocky slopes on acid soil, rather local. June — September.

2   Woodruff   *Galium odoratum*   **Rubiaceae**
The tiny white flowers, four-lobed and funnel-shaped, grow in loose heads at the end of the long, straggling stem which has whorls of six to nine lance-shaped leaves at intervals, like green ruffs. They have tiny forward-pointing prickles. The plants, which are perennial, grow quickly with rooting stems and form spreading green mats. They have a pleasant scent like new-mown hay when dried, and were formerly used in linen-cupboards and chests to freshen them and keep moths away. The small fruits have hooked bristles.

Woods and copses, often in beechwoods. May — June.

1.

2.

PLATE 18

1   Greater Bindweed, Hedge Bindweed *Calystegia sepium* **Convolvulaceae**
The large white flowers are solitary on long axillary stalks, and have an epicalyx of two heart-shaped bracts covering the calyx. The leaves are large, smooth and narrow-shaped. The stem twists and twines round any support it can find, while the long white underground stems are difficult to eradicate if it becomes a garden weed. There are sub-species with pink and white striped flowers found near gardens.

Banks, hedges. July — September.

2   Enchanter's Nightshade *Circaea lutetiana* **Onagraceae**
The thin, bright green, heart-shaped leaves, paler beneath, are in pairs along the erect main stem; both leaf stalks and stems are reddish. The leaves taper towards the tip and are minutely and distantly toothed. The flowers are in a spike-like inflorescence held well above the leaves, small, white, with two petals which are narrow and divided for half their length. They have two stamens and the stigma is two-lobed. The pale greenish sepals are tinged with red and are reflexed. The flower buds are bright pink. The plant spreads rapidly by slender branched far-creeping rhizomes. (The figured specimen is possibly the Hybrid Enchanter's Nightshade, *C.* x *intermedia, C. alpina* x *C. lutetiana*.)

Woods and shady places. June — August.

3   Spring Beauty *Claytonia perfoliata* **syn.** *Montia perfoliata* **Portulaceae**
A glabrous and fleshy annual with long-stalked basal leaves. The stem-leaves are joined in a pair, forming a shallow concave 'saucer' around the inflorescence of five-petalled, glistening white flowers. An introduced plant (native of North America) it is now locally abundant and very invasive. There is also a pink form, equally invasive.

Light, sandy, open ground. May — July

4   Black Bindweed *Fallopia convolvulus* **syn.** *Polygonum convolvulus* **Polygonaceae**
A scrambling annual, sometimes twining and climbing, with angular, somewhat mealy stems. The leaves are stalked, triangular with cordate bases, smooth and green above and mealy beneath. The greenish-white flower clusters are in the axils of the leaves. The outer flower segments are narrowly winged and enlarge in fruit.

It is a common weed of arable land, gardens and waste places. July — October.

Plate 19

1   White Dead-nettle   *Lamium album*   **Labiatae**

Perennial, hairy, with a creeping rhizome and square-stalked erect stems. The large, creamy-white flowers are in whorls spaced along the stems, with two large, rough, oval-heart-shaped leaves, coarsely toothed, below each whorl. The high arched hood of the flower conceals six black stamens set in pairs. The calyx is tubular ending in six sharp points and is black at the base.

Waste ground, hedge banks, but less common in the north and west. May – November.

2   Common Hemp-nettle   *Galeopsis tetrahit*   **Labiatae**

This is an annual, very similar to the pink form described under 'Red and Pink Flowers' but the flowers are white with purple markings on the lower lip, and it is less common.

Hedge banks, woods. July – September.

3   Gipsy-wort   *Lycopus europaeus*   **Labiatae**

A perennial with creeping rhizome and stiff, erect stems. It is rather like mint but has no scent. The tiny, bell-shaped flowers are in tight whorls spaced along the stem, they are white with a few small purple dots on the lower lip, and are set in the axils of a pair of oval to lance-shaped leaves, short-stalked, deeply and sharply toothed.

River banks, marshes, ditches, damp places. Mostly in the south but less common in Scotland. June – September.

1.

2.

3.

PLATE 20

1   Shepherd's Purse   *Capsella bursa-pastoris*   **Cruciferae**
Usually annual. A common weed of gardens and cultivated land. The erect stems rise from a rosette of entire or sometimes pinnately-lobed leaves, which are stalked. The stem leaves are narrower, arrow-shaped and clasping. The flowers are small, white, and at first in a close cluster at the end of the stem, but as the fruits develop the stem lengthens, spacing them out, and the characteristic heart-shaped 'purses' are noticeable.

Most of the year.

2   Jack-by the hedge, Hedge Garlic   *Alliaria petiolata*   **Cruciferae**
A tall plant with erect stem and tap-root, it smells strongly of garlic. The small white, four-petalled flowers are in a close cluster, and are soon succeeded by the long stiff narrow pods, which curve upwards. The stem leaves are heart-shaped with pointed teeth and short stalks; the rosette leaves are long-stalked and kidney-shaped. The stems are sparsely hairy above, and below they are thickly covered with white hairs.

Very common on hedge-banks and wood margins. April – June.

PLATE 21

1   Smith's Pepperwort   *Lepidium heterophyllum*   Cruciferae

Perennial. The ascending stems curve upwards in an open circle from the stout woody root-stock. They are closely set with clasping, narrowly triangular, toothed leaves which are softly hairy and have long pointed basal lobes. The rather flat flower-head at the top of the stem is closely packed with small white flowers, but the stem elongates as the fruits ripen, spacing them out. These are flat with the style protruding at the tip, and the fruit-stalk is hairy.

On dry banks and roadsides, also arable fields. May − August.

2   Alpine or Mountain Scurvy Grass
    Cochlearia pyrenaica* ssp. *alpina*   Cruciferae   syn. *Cochlearia officinalis* ssp. *alpina

Biennial to perennial, with a long slender tap-root and one or more procumbent or ascending glabrous shoots. The basal leaves are small, dark green, cordate and stalked, the upper ones are more or less sessile. The white petals are two or three times as long as the sepals and narrow abruptly into a thin claw, revealing the short green sepals. The ripe fruit is elliptical, tapering at both ends.

Local, wet rock-ledges and by streamlets on Scottish mountains, also Hebrides, Orkney and Shetland. June − August.

3   Common Scurvy Grass   *Cochlearia officinalis* ssp. *officinalis*   Cruciferae

A glabrous perennial plant with branching, procumbent or ascending flowering shoots, and shiny, dark green, fleshy leaves, rounded and slightly lobed, which are cordate and long-stalked at the base. The stem leaves are stalkless and have small basal auricles, they are often more pointed or ivy-shaped nearer the top of the stem. The flowers are stalked and have four white petals, widely spaced, and four fleshy green sepals. At first they are in close clusters at the end of the stem, but as the rounded fruits develop the stem lengthens, spacing them more widely apart. The buds are sometimes tinged with pink. It is widespread and abundant all round the coast. Formerly eaten by sailors especially, its pleasantly sharp-tasting leaves are a valuable source of ascorbic acid (Vitamin C).

May − August.

1.

2.

3.

3.

PLATE 22

1 Wavy Bitter-cress *Cardamine flexuosa* Cruciferae

An erect, slender biennial with wavy stems. The few basal leaves are in a loose rosette, with five pairs of rounded leaflets, the terminal leaflet larger, the leaflets on the upper leaves narrower. The tiny white petals are twice as long as the sepals, and there are usually six stamens. The fruits are narrow, set on slender upward curving stalks. A common plant of moist shady places and by streams. The annual *Cardamine hirsuta* is similar but smaller with more basal leaves, straight stems, and four pale stamens.

Common on bare ground, screes and walls. Both, April — September.

2 Field Penny-cress *Thlaspi arvense* Cruciferae

Annual or over-wintering with a slender tap-root and one or more erect leafy stems. The stem leaves are lance-shaped with slightly toothed margins, stalkless, clasping the stem with short lobes. The basal leaves are broadly oblong narrowing to a stalked base, they are not in a rosette. The inflorescence of tiny white flowers lengthens greatly in fruit, and the large rounded flat fruits are very conspicuous, their broad wings curving at the top to a deep narrow notch which contains the almost invisible short style.

Although a doubtful native it is a common weed of arable land and waste ground. May — July.

3 Thale Cress *Arabidopsis thaliana* Cruciferae

An annual, occasionally biennial, with a slender flower-stem, which has a few clasping leaves, and rises from a basal rosette of short-stalked, oval, hairy leaves often reddish in colour. The tiny white flowers are clustered at the top of the stem which lengthens as the long narrow seed-pods develop. In large plants the stem is branched.

The specimen shown is from dry sandy dunes and is typical of this habitat — and a dry garden! March — April.

PLATE 23

1   Bogbean   *Menyanthes trifoliata*   **Menyanthaceae**
The thick fleshy aquatic or creeping rhizomes bear erect, long-stalked trifoliate leaves with smooth, untoothed, oval leaflets. The leafless flower-stem carries a raceme of very beautiful, conspicuously fringed flowers, which are five-lobed, star-shaped, pinkish outside and white within. The fruit is a shiny green oval capsule.

Wet bogs, ponds, edges of small lochs. May — July.

2   Water Crowfoot   *Ranunculus aquatilis*   **Ranunculaceae**
The branching stems normally carry two types of leaves: the submerged leaves, which are finely cut into thread-like segments, and the floating leaves, which are deeply cut into broad, straight-sided lobes. The white buttercup-like flowers have five petals, yellow at the base, and are solitary on erect stalks. This is one of a group of white-flowered aquatic buttercups which are not always easy to tell apart.

Ponds, ditches and streams. May — June.

3   Ivy-leaved Water Crowfoot   *Ranunculus hederaceus*   **Ranunculaceae**
The branching stem creeps in the mud or has the upper part floating. The leaves, usually opposite, are stalked, rounded with broad-based lobes, sometimes with dark basal markings. The small white flowers have narrow petals scarcely exceeding the sepals.

Shallow water and its muddy margins. June — September.

1.

2.

3.

PLATE 24

1   Narrow-leaved Helleborine   *Cephalanthera longifolia*   **Orchidaceae**
The tall stem has whitish basal sheaths and long, narrow, lance-shaped leaves further
up, often folded with drooping tips. The upper ones are often longer than the
flower-spike. The flowers are pure white, much longer than their bracts except for
the lowest ones. They have a small orange spot at the lip-base, and the outer
perianth segments are pointed.

*Woods and shady places, especially on calcareous soils, but local and rare. As far north as
W. Ross, Inverness and the Inner Hebrides. May – July.*

2   Coral-root Orchid   *Corallorhiza trifida*   **Orchidaceae**
Small and inconspicuous, with a slender, yellowish-green glabrous stem with two to
four long, brown, sheathing scales reaching to about half-way up the stem. The small
flowers are in a loose raceme, with very small bracts, the outer segments curving
down and yellowish green; the white lip is broadly oblong, slightly three-lobed and
prominent. The plant is saprophytic, without leaves, and has a pale, creamy, coral-
like rhizome, much branched and fleshy.

*Damp peaty or mossy woods, especially of birch, pine or alder, and moist dune-slacks, but rare.
North to Inverness and Ross. June – August.*

3   Creeping Lady's Tresses   *Goodyera repens*   **Orchidaceae**
The creeping rhizome has slender stolons ending in rosettes of oval evergreen
leaves, which have five strongly-marked parallel veins with a network of small veins
between. The stem is erect with the upper part sheathed in pale bract-like leaves,
and ends in a twisted one-sided spike of creamy-white fragrant flowers, each with
a large hood, two downward pointing lateral segments, and a narrow lip.

Locally in pine woods. July – August.

PLATE 25

1   Greater Butterfly Orchid   *Platanthera chlorantha*   Orchidaceae

The tall stem up to 45cm smooth and erect, has two clasping, unspotted, oval, blunt leaves, near its base. The flowers are spread out in a long pyramidal spike; each flower has a narrow bract beneath, and is greenish-white and sweetly scented, especially at night. The upper perianth segments form a small hood, the two side sepals being narrow, pointed, and spread horizontally, and the undivided lip is strap-shaped and points down. The spur is very long, curving down and forward. The two pollinia (pollen masses) slope forwards and outwards, diverging from 2mm apart at the base to 4mm at the tips. Pollination is by moths to whose heads the pollinia become attached and are carried to the next flower.

Woods, scrub, grassy slopes, especially on base-rich soil. June — July.

2   Lesser Butterfly Orchid   *Platanthera bifolia*   Orchidaceae

Similar to the Butterfly Orchid, but rather smaller; the flower-spike and the flowers are rather narrower. The flowers are more creamy-white with a slender, horizontal spur, and the pollinia vertical and parallel. It is less common.

Open woods and fens, grassy and heathy places, on base-rich soil. Both found in fields on the West Coast, Loch Carron area. June — July.

3   Small White Orchid   *Pseudorchis albida*   Orchidaceae

Small, erect and slender, with narrow unspotted leaves up the stem. The flower-spike is very narrow, dense and cylindrical, with tiny greenish, creamy-white pendulous flowers and broader bracts which give it a leafy appearance. The vanilla-scented flowers hang down, looking almost bell-shaped; the lip is three-lobed and the spur is very short.

Grass-land on hills and mountains. Local. June — July.

1.

1.

2.

3.

PLATE 26

1   (Scots) Lovage   *Ligusticum scoticum*   Umbelliferae
A perennial plant of medium height, with smooth, slightly branching stems that turn red at the base, as do the sheaths at the junction of leaf and stem. The leaves are twice trifoliate, broad, toothed and shiny green. The greenish-white flowers are in rather small close umbels and are five-lobed, with purple anthers. The plant is celery-scented and can be used as a pot-herb.

On rocky coasts. July.

2   Spignel, Meu, Baldmoney   *Meum athamanticum*   Umbelliferae
The very finely-cut, lacy, aromatic leaves have whorls of hair-like leaflets and long stalks, giving this perennial plant a green feathery appearance. The slender flower-stalks carry umbels of small white flowers followed by egg-shaped fruits with sharp ridges.

Grassy places on mountains, local, north to Argyll and Aberdeen. Also cultivated in gardens. June – August.

PLATE 27

1   Pignut, Earthnut   *Conopodium majus*   Umbelliferae
A slender, erect perennial with smooth hollow stems narrowing towards the base, and rising some way below the soil surface from a hard, irregular, brown-skinned and white-fleshed edible tuber. Both stem and basal leaves are lacy in appearance, finely divided into small narrow leaflets, and they wither very soon. The white-flowered umbels are small, nodding in bud, and the small fruits are narrowly egg-shaped.

Fields, roadsides, woods. May — June.

2   Myrrh, Sweet Cicely   *Myrrhis odorata*   Umbelliferae
Perennial, tall, sturdy, bushy and pleasantly aromatic, with slightly grooved, hollow stems and very large, spreading, pinnately-divided, fern-like leaves which usually have silvery patches and are pale underneath. The flowers are white and are followed by long, ridged fruits, green at first, later shining blackish-brown; they are erect. It is a doubtful native, but well established, and may possibly have spread from old herb gardens, where it was grown for its aniseed flavour.

Grassy places, hedges and woods. May — July.

3. Caraway, Carvie   *Carum carvi*   Umbelliferae
A slender, erect biennial, with much-divided leaves, those on the stems having linear leaflets. The flower-heads are small, with rounded, creamy-white petals. It is rather rare when wild, growing on grassy banks, but is grown in herb gardens for the aromatic seeds, brown and ribbed when ripe, which are used for flavouring. They give a distinctive flavour to cakes and biscuits and to cheese. It was very popular as a culinary plant formerly and is still in use. Originally it was brought from Europe.

June — July.

PLATE 28

1   Bishopweed, Ground Elder   *Aegopodium podagraria*   Umbelliferae
A perennial with stout, hollow, grooved stems and far-reaching rhizomes which are white when young. The long-stalked triangular leaves are usually divided into three groups of three, broadly oval, pointed leaflets. The white flowers, in umbels are followed by flattened oval fruits.

Waste ground, and an all-too-common garden weed. May — July.

2   Sanicle   *Sanicula europaea*   Umbelliferae
An erect and hairless perennial with long-stalked, shiny, basal leaves which have five rounded and sharply toothed lobes. The stem leaves are smaller. The tiny white or pinkish flowers are in small, few-flowered, closely packed umbels. The oval fruits are covered with hooked bristles.

A woodland plant, especially beech-woods on lime. North to Caithness, except on poor soils. May — August.

3   Fool's Parsley   *Aethusa cynapium*   Umbelliferae
An annual which is distinguished by the numerous narrow bracteoles hanging down from the umbels. It is a tall hairless plant with finely divided leaves and is very poisonous. The flowers have unequal petals; the fruits are oval with broad ridges.

A weed of cultivated ground, but mostly in the south and absent from the north of Scotland. July — August.

PLATE 29

1   Cow Parsley, Queen Anne's Lace   *Anthriscus sylvestris*   Umbelliferae
Tall, erect perennial, downy, with hollow furrowed stems, and numerous fresh green, fern-like leaves which enhance the umbels of pure white flowers. These are followed by smooth, oval fruits. This is one of the commonest plants of this family, it edges roadsides nearly everywhere with the white froth of its lacy flowers in early summer.

June – July.

2   Hemlock Water Dropwort   *Oenanthe crocata*   Umbelliferae
A tall, sturdy, erect perennial, with hollow grooved stems. It is very poisonous. The large 3–4 pinnate leaves have broad wedge-shaped toothed segments. The white flowers are in umbels six to eight inches wide with numerous bracts when young.

Wet places. Mainly in the south and west. June – July.

PLATE 30

1   Greater Burnet Saxifrage   *Pimpinella major*   Umbelliferae
A perennial of medium height with a hairless, strongly ridged stem. The uppermost stem leaves are narrow and divided with sheathing petioles but the pinnate basal leaves are much larger with broad, oval, coarsely toothed leaflets. The umbels are terminal, with no bracts or bracteoles. The flowers are white, sometimes pink, and have long stamens.

Roadsides, wood edges, rare in the north. June — July.

2   Wild Carrot   *Daucus carota* ssp. *carota*   Umbelliferae
An erect, branched, hairy biennial, with a solid, ridged stem. The leaves are tri-pinnate, with rather broadly oval and pointed leaflets. The umbels are crowded and have large bracts with linear or 3-forked segments which form a ruff below. The central flower of the umbel is often red. The fruit is oval, with spiny ridges. As the fruit ripens the umbel becomes strongly concave, closing up into a tight basket-like head.

Fields, dunes and grassy places, abundant near the sea and on chalky soils. June — August.

PLATE 31

1   Hogweed, Cow Parsnip   *Heracleum sphondylium*   **Umbelliferae**
Tall, robust, with ridged stems that are hollow, and have downward
pointing hairs. The leaves are large and rough, grey-green, with clasping
bases, and lobed and coarsely toothed leaflets, the lower leaves being
stalked. The white flowers are unusual in size, the outer ones being larger,
and the petals are notched. The bractioles of the umbels are narrow and
turn down. The fruits are long, oval, flattened and smooth.

Up to 3m. Very common, roadsides, grassy places. June — September.

2   Giant Hogweed   *Heracleum mantegazzianum*   **Umbelliferae**
A native of the Caucasus, the Giant Hogweed is now naturalised in several places
near rivers and in waste ground. It is the largest of the family, easily recognised
by its enormous size, up to 5 m. in height. It should not be handled as it can
produce a painful rash.

June — September.

1.

2.

Plate 32

1 Ramsons *Allium ursinum* Liliaceae

The star-like flowers are in a loose cluster of about twelve at the end of a smooth stalk which is triangular in section. They are enclosed while in bud by two membranous spathes. The large, flat, glossy leaves are long-stalked, broadly oval and pointed, smooth and bright green. Like *A. paradoxum* the plant smells strongly of garlic.

Damp woods and shady places, growing in masses and covering large stretches of ground. May − June.

2 Few-flowered Leek *Allium paradoxum* Liliaceae

Not native but where naturalised it grows very plentifully. The stem is smooth and triangular in section, at its end are two papery bracts surrounding a cluster of pale green bulbils, and one or two (seldom more) long stalks emerge from this cluster, one with a flower with six white, rather transparent petals and six stamens. The other stalk bears two or more papery bracts and another small cluster of bulbils. The single leaf is long and narrow, and clasps the flower-stem at the base.

Woods, shady places. May − June.

1.

2.

PLATE 33

1   Crow Garlic, Wild Onion   *Allium vineale*   **Liliaceae**

Bulb with off-sets. The umbel is composed of small green bulbils almost hidden by their interlacing thread-like ends, and occasionally with a few flowers. These are bell-shaped, white with green stripes, long-stalked, with protruding stamens. The umbel is partly concealed by a rounded dry, papery spathe with a short beak. The leaves are long, rounded, hollow, slightly grooved, and very narrow.

Fields, roadsides, local but as far north as Aberdeen. June − July.

2   Field Garlic   *Allium oleraceum*   **Liliaceae**

The bulb usually has off-sets. The umbel is loose, with brownish bulbils, and several bell-shaped flowers, with unequal stalks, white with green stripes, and stamens which only reach the tips of the petals. The spathe is two-valved, with very long, narrow points.

Dry, grassy places, mostly east, north to Moray. July − August.

3   Scottish Asphodel   *Tofieldia palustris*   **Liliaceae**

From a small rhizome the short, rigid, sword-shaped leaves rise in small tufts. The tall, thin flower stem, with sometimes a much smaller stem-leaf, ends in a short, dense raceme of tiny white or greenish-white flowers. The whole plant is tiny and easily overlooked.

By springs and streams on mountains, local. June − August.

1.

2

3.

2.

PLATE 34

1   Dog Rose   *Rosa canina*   **Rosaceae**

The commonest and most widespread of our native wild roses, and one of the most beautiful. The delicate flowers, in white and varying shades of pink, cover the bushes along country roadsides in June and July, and later in autumn the bright red hips make a brilliant and cheering display till winter. The calyx is distinctive, the five long sepals in three patterns, two being bearded, two smooth-edged, and the fifth bearded on one side only. This gave rise to ancient rhyming riddles, such as:

> 'Of us five brothers at the same time born,
> Two from our birthday ever beards have worn,
> On other two none ever have appeared,
> While our fifth brother wears but half a beard.'

The sepals are not persistent, and fall early. The stems are prickly, with curved thorns. Another very similar rose is common in the north, the Downy Rose, *R. sherardi,* but the leaves are densely downy and the flowers are usually a deeper pink. It prefers calcareous soil.

2   Sweet Briar   *Rosa rubiginosa*   **Rosaceae**

This is deliciously scented; the leaflets are glandular, providing the scent which spreads in the air, especially after rain. The flowers are usually a deeper pink than *R. canina.* The sepals are persistent, remaining on the red hips. It is commonest in the south, rare in the north, prefers a calcareous soil, and can grow into a large tall bush, flowering in June and July. It is a delightful rose to grow by the door, to enjoy the scent as you go in and out.

1.

2.

PLATE 35

1   Water Aven   *Geum rivale*   Rosaceae

The short thick rhizome gives rise to long-stalked leaves and the rather longer flower stems, all softly hairy. These basal leaves are pinnate with several pairs of unequal leaflets and a large rounded and lobed terminal leaflet. The flower stem leaves are small, divided or simple, with narrow stipules at the base. The drooping bell-shaped flowers have a purplish calyx and epicalyx, and the petals are orange-pink. In fruit the flower-stalk becomes erect and the short piece between calyx and the dense head of the carpels lengthens; the styles are long and hooked, giving the seed-head a 'pin-cushion' appearance.

Marshy ground, stream sides, usually in shade. May — September.

2   Marsh Cinquefoil   *Potentilla palustris*   Rosaceae

This is another perennial, moisture-loving plant with a woody, creeping rhizome and long, leafy, ascending stems which die back nearly to the base in winter. The lower leaves are pinnate, with from five to seven leaflets, oval, pointed and sharply toothed, with large stipules. The upper leaves are smaller, sometimes trifoliate. The flowers are in loose, terminal clusters, dark purplish red and having wide sepals, longer and wider than the petals, which are quite tiny and narrow. Stamens, carpels, and styles are all deep purple.

Bogs, marshes, wet heaths and moors. May — July.

PLATE 36

1   Red Clover   *Trifolium pratense*   **Leguminosae**

Mostly erect or spreading, with strong stems. The stem leaves have pale green triangular stipules with a bristle-like point; the basal leaves long stalks; all have three large leaflets usually with a whitish crescent. The flowers are in a close rounded head and are rose in colour.

Grassy places. May — September.

2   Zigzag Clover   *Trifolium medium*   **Leguminosae**

The flower-heads are deeper in colour and the florets are longer and more pointed. The leaflets are narrow and dark green, usually without a distinct whitish mark. The stem is wavy. The free part of the stipules is awl-shaped and spreading.

Also in grassy places and edges of fields, commoner in the north. June — September.

PLATE 37

1 Hare's Foot Clover   *Trifolium arvense*   **Leguminosae**
A soft downy annual, branching and more or less erect. The tiny flowers are almost hidden in the downy heads, and are pale pink, narrow and scarcely seem to open. The flower-heads are at first rounded and gradually lengthen. The hairy calyx-teeth are longer than the petals, giving the head its furry appearance. The trefoil leaves are narrow and at the base of the leaf stalk there are two pinkish stipules ending in sharp points.

Sandy fields, pastures and dunes. June — September.

2 Soft Trefoil, Knotted Clover   *Trifolium striatum*   **Leguminosae**
A downy, often procumbent annual. The oval, unstalked flower-heads are more or less enfolded in the large stipules of the subtending leaves when young. The stipules are ovate or triangular with long narrow points. The downy calyx-tubes of the pink flowers become inflated in fruit.

Dry, open sandy places, usually calcareous, very local, north to Kincardineshire. May — July.

3 Rough Clover   *Trifolium scabrum*   **Leguminosae**
Annual. This resembles *T. striatum* but is not so tall. The flowers are very tiny and whitish, and the ribbed calyx does not become inflated, but has outward-curving teeth. The whole plant is downy.

Dry places on shallow and sandy soils, but not in the north. May — July.

4 Alsike Clover   *Trifolium hybridum*   **Leguminosae**
The flower-heads are smaller than those of the red clovers on the preceding plate, and the flowers are pink or pinkish-white, with short stalks. The leaves have no white markings but have small oblong stipules with pointed tips. Not a native but now well naturalised.

Roadsides, and also grown for fodder. June — September.

5 Strawberry Clover   *Trifolium fragiferum*   **Leguminosae**
A smooth, creeping perennial rooting at the nodes, with pink flowers and a hairy calyx which swells in fruit to form an inflated, round, pinkish, two-lipped receptacle for the seeds. The pointed whitish stipules are long, sheathing the stem at the nodes.

Grassy places mainly on heavy clay soils but not in the north. May — July.

1.

2.

3.

4.

5.

PLATE 38

1   Bush Vetch   *Vicia sepium*   Leguminosae
The pale rosy-purple flowers, almost sessile, are in small clusters of about two to six in the axils of the leaves; each has the petals veined with darker lines and a hairy tubular calyx with unequal teeth. The seed-pods are black when ripe. The leaves have around six pairs of oval leaflets with the leaf-stalk ending in a branched tendril, and there are small stipules at the junction of leaf and stem.

Common on roadside banks, hedgerows, where it spreads in a tangled mass. April — October.

2   Bitter Vetch   *Lathyrus linifolius*   syn. *Lathyrus montanus*   Leguminosae
The rosy-purple flowers, two to four, are loosely spaced on a slender stem; as they fade they turn to greenish-blue. The calyx teeth are unequal, the lower being longer. There are two to four pairs of sharply pointed, lance-shaped leaflets, and the leaf-stalk ends in a point, not a tendril. The stipules are also sharply pointed.

Hedge-banks, heaths and hilly country, commoner in the west and north. April — July.

1.

2.

PLATE 39

1   Restharrow   *Ononis repens*   **Leguminosae**
Procumbent, with many spreading branches which are hairy, and have many small oval leaflets, hairy and slightly notched. The large pink flowers are in short leafy spikes. The similar, but upright, Ononis spinosa, is rare in Scotland.

Dry sandy and grassy places, coastal dunes. July — September.

2   Narrow-leaved Vetch   *Vicia sativa* **ssp.** *angustifolia*   **Leguminosae**
A slender scrambling plant with bright rosy flowers usually in pairs in the axils of the leaves. These have several pairs of narrow, blunt or pointed leaflets and end in branched tendrils. The pods are long and narrow.

Banks, hedges, dry grassy places. May — September.

3   Common Vetch   *Vicia sativa* **ssp.** *sativa*   **Leguminosae**
A larger plant which can be trailing, scrambling or erect. The leaflets are linear to obovate, blunt with a short narrow point. The flowers, rosy-purple, are single or in pairs, in the leaf axils. The plant is often slightly hairy. Intermediates between this and ssp. *angustifolia* can occur.

Grassy places, hedge-banks, scrub. May — September.

1.

2.

3.

PLATE 40

1   Bloody Cranesbill   *Geranium sanguineum*   Geraniaceae

The large bright purple-crimson flowers of this bushy perennial make brilliant patches of colour, often in the grassy hollows along the tops of sea cliffs. The flowers are usually solitary on long stalks, and the dark green leaves are deeply cut into five to seven lobes which are themselves further divided. The characteristic 'stork's-bill' seed-heads are specially noticeable in autumn before the carpels roll up to release the seeds.

Grasslands, woods, rocks, cliff-tops and fixed dunes. July — August.

2   Herb Robert   *Geranium robertianum*   Geraniaceae

The reddish hairy stems are spreading and more or less erect, bearing palmate leaves divided to the base with the leaflets further divided. These often turn bright red as they age, and the whole plant has a strong smell. The small flowers have five petals, pink with deeper veins, and the anthers are orange or purple.

Woods, banks, old walls, very common. April — October.

3   Shining Cranesbill   *Geranium lucidum*   Geraniaceae

An annual with branching, ascending, red stems, rather brittle and fleshy. The glossy green leaves have long stalks and are often red-tinged. They have five to seven lobes widening above and hairless, but only divided to one-half or three-quarters of the leaf. The flowers are small and pink, petals not notched.

Shady banks, dry grassland, dunes. In the south and rare in the north. May — August.

4   Long-stalked Cranesbill   *Geranium columbinum*   Geraniaceae

A slender annual with erect branches. The slightly hairy basal leaves have long stalks and are divided almost to the base into five to seven narrow pinnate lobes. The upper leaves are smaller, on shorter stalks and somewhat less lobed. The purplish-pink flowers have rounded petals, sometimes with a few small teeth at the apex, and the hairy pointed sepals are tipped with a bristle.

Open dry grassland and scrub, rather local and mainly in the south-east but north to Angus. June — July.

1.

2.

3.

4.

PLATE 41

1   Dove's-foot Cranesbill   *Geranium molle*   **Geraniaceae**
An annual, branched from the base, with spreading or ascending stems, all clothed with long soft white hairs. The lower leaves are rounded and lobed with long stalks. The upper leaves are smaller and more sharply lobed. The rosy-purple petals are deeply notched at the tips, the sepals are hairy, and the flower-stalks turn upwards as the beaked fruit ripens.

April — September.

2   Cut-leaved Cranesbill   *Geranium dissectum*   **Geraniaceae**
A rather straggling annual with hairy stems. The long-stalked basal leaves resemble those of Geranium molle but are much more deeply cut. The petals of the rose-pink flowers are slightly notched.

Cultivated and waste ground, grassland, hedgebanks. May — August.

3   Common Storksbill   *Erodium circutarium* **agg. Geraniaceae**
This annual is variable in habit but mostly spreading and branching, usually hairy and sticky. The leaves are pinnate, with pinnately cut leaflets and conspicuous whitish pointed stipules. The rosy-purple flowers are in a loose umbel, sometimes with a blackish spot at the base of each of the two upper petals. The hairy carpels have beaks which twist spirally when ripe.

Dunes, grassland, sandy places. June — September.

4   Dwarf Mallow   *Malva neglecta*   **Malvaceae**
A prostrate and densely downy annual or biennial, with long-stalked rounded, lobed leaves, and flowers in small clusters along the stems. The square-ended petals are pale pinkish-lilac or white with lilac veins, and are more than twice as long as the calyx. Outside each calyx is an additional calyx-like structure – the epicalyx.

Waste ground, roadsides, beaches, more frequent in the south. June — September.

1.

2.

3.

4.

PLATE 42

1   Musk Mallow   *Malva moschata*   Malvaceae
The erect stems, of medium height, are slightly hairy, sometimes purple-spotted, and branch out from the stock. The long-stalked basal leaves are kidney-shaped with three shallow lobes which have crenate margins. The stem leaves are deeply cut into narrow segments, variable but often lacy in appearance; they have two small pointed stipules. The flowers, solitary in the axils of the leaves, and in a terminal cluster, are delicate rose-pink, shining, with waved, rather square ends to the petals. They have five wide, pointed sepals with an epicalyx of three smaller lobes, forming a cup. The sepals persist in fruit, surrounding the nutlets, which are blackish when ripe.

Grassy places, pastures, hedge-banks. July — August.

2   Common Mallow   *Malva sylvestris*   Malvaceae
Also of medium height, the stems are ascending or decumbent, with sparse hairs. The long-stalked basal leaves are rounded with usually five crenate lobes, heart-shaped at base. The stem leaves are similar but smaller, with fringed stipules. The stalked flowers rise from the leaf axils along the stem; they are mauve-pink veined with darker red. The petals are deeply notched at the tips and are longer than the sepals and the small epicalyx segments. The nutlets are brownish green when ripe.

Roadsides, waste ground, but less common in the north. June — September.

1.

2.

1.

PLATE 43

1   Lesser Knapweed, Hardheads   *Centaurea nigra*   **Compositae**
The thistle-like heads are at the ends of branching stems, which swell just below the flower-head. The involucre is made up of small bracts, dark brown or nearly black, edged with black, hair-like teeth, and over-lapping closely. The leaves are lance-shaped, narrow and rough, stalkless on the stems, those from the base being stalked, sparsely toothed and much longer.

Roadsides and grassy banks. July — September.

2   Great Knapweed   *Centaurea scabiosa*   **Compositae**
This is a larger plant with handsome flower-heads which have a showy outer ring of large florets. The bracts surrounding the flower-head are green, with a blackish-brown fringe. The leaves on the stems are small and stalkless; the basal leaves are large, stalked and deeply pinnatifid, the lobes sometimes slightly toothed. The stems are branching, grooved and hairy.

Dry grassland, roadside banks, especially on limestone. South Scotland, and also in Sutherland, where a white form has been found. July — September.

1.

2.

PLATE 44

1   Hemp Agrimony   *Eupatorium cannabinum*   **Compositae**

A large, leafy plant, medium tall with stiff, erect, woody stems that are downy and reddish, and short branches bearing at their heads thick, flat-headed clusters (corymbs) of mauve-pink scented flowers. These have a feathery appearance due to the long styles emerging like threads from the groups of small, tubular florets, surrounded by their purple-tipped bracts. The leaves are mostly divided into three segments, lance-shaped and coarsely toothed, opposite and gland-spotted. The basal leaves are stalked.

Marshes and fens, stream-banks and moist woods, but not common in Scotland. July – September.

2   Lesser Burdock   *Arctium minus*   **Compositae**

The red-purple, thistle-like flower-heads are closely set, in racemes or corymbs, both at the head of the stem, and in the axils of the stem leaves, the groups of tubular florets surrounded by bracts which have long hooked tips. The branching stems are furrowed, often reddish and rather woolly. The leaves are oval, stalked, deeply veined and sparsely cottony, the leaf-stalks (petioles) of the basal leaves hollow, distinguishing this from the Great Burdock, *Arctium lappa*, (not a Scottish native).

July – September.

1.

2.

PLATE 45

1　Melancholy Thistle　*Cirsium heterophyllum*　Compositae

A tall, handsome plant with large solitary heads of red-purple flowers which have adpressed bracts, long, narrow and purplish-tipped. The erect stems are grooved and cottony, but not winged. The leaves are flat, soft and green above, thickly white-felted beneath; the upper ones clasp the stem, but the basal leaves are very large, broad at the base, toothed, and tapering upwards sometimes dividing into narrow lobes. It is without prickles, and is a plant of stream-sides and damp areas in high ground and mountains, where the large clumps are spectacular.

July – August.

2　Spear Thistle, Scottish Thistle　*Cirsium vulgare*　Compositae

This is the true Scottish thistle, as depicted on some of the earliest Scottish coins, as, for example, the James VI 2-merk piece or thistle dollar of 1579. The flower heads are large, the rounded purple plume of tiny flowers emerging from the spiny green involucre which is slightly cottony and narrows noticeably at the top. The stems are erect, spiny-winged, cottony and furrowed. The leaves are all deeply cut and waved, lobes and teeth and tipped with sharp spines; they are hairy above and cottony beneath. A large, well-grown plant is extremely handsome, even majestic in appearance, such as one often finds on the west coast, and is well fitted to be the national emblem.

July – October.

1.

2.

PLATE 46

1   Slender Thistle   *Carduus tenuiflorus*   **Compositae**
Annual or biennial, with a stout tap-root and erect stems which have broad and uninterrupted spiny wings. The stem leaves are narrow with wavy spinous margins: the basal leaves blunt, rather small, narrow and spinous; all are somewhat cottony beneath. The flower-heads are in dense terminal clusters, with the stem winged close beneath them; they are narrow with lance shaped bracts ending in an outward-curving spine.

Waysides and waste places, especially by the sea. June – August.

2   Creeping Thistle   *Cirsium arvense*   **Compositae**
The rather small flower-heads are in loose clusters, each long-stalked and rising from the axil of a leaf. The flowers are lilac with deeper purple involucres. The leaves clasp the unwinged stem and are lance-shaped, deeply cut and spiny.

The plant spreads rapidly by creeping white roots and is a weed of fields and cultivated ground, as well as being common on waste land. June – August.

3   Welted Thistle   *Carduus crispus* **syn.** *Carduus acanthoides*   **Compositae**
Tall biennial with a slender tap-root and erect cottony stem which has narrow, wavy, spinous-margined wings, apart from just beneath the flower-head. The stem leaves are deeply cut with three-lobed spiny segments; the basal leaves narrow to a stalk at the base; all are cottony beneath. The flower-heads are large (up to 3cm), and almost round, with long bracts ending in a slender spine, and usually in dense clusters of three to five.

Damp grass verges, burnsides. Common in the south, becoming rare in the north. June – August.

PLATE 47

1   Milk Thistle   *Silybum marianum*   Compositae
A tall striking annual or biennial plant. The stems are erect, strong, unwinged and slightly cottony, with clasping stem leaves which have spiny margins. The basal leaves are very large, narrowing into an unstalked base, with strong spines on their edges. All are shiny green with prominent white margins to the veins. The rosy-purple flower-heads are solitary, erect or somewhat drooping, and are fiercely armed with long sharp spiny bracts.

An introduced plant but naturalised in waste places locally as far north as Easter Ross. June – August.

2   Marsh Thistle   *Cirsium palustre*   Compositae
A biennial of medium height, with erect, sturdy, furrowed stems, which are narrowly but continuously winged, spiny, hairy and cottony. The decurrent stem leaves are narrow and long with wavy, spine-tipped lobes. The basal leaves, appearing as a flat rosette in the first year, are stalked and also lobed and spiny. The flower-heads are in densely crowded clusters at the ends of the main stem and short ascending branches rising from the leaf axils. The florets are red-purple, occasionally white, and their bracts are purplish, narrow and sharply tipped.

Marshes, damp grass-land, open woods. Very common. July – September.

1.

2.

PLATE 48

1   Butterbur   *Petasites hybridus*   Compositae
This is the native plant, distinguished by its pink flowers; the similar, but introduced white form, *P. albus*, is common in the north. Both are perennial and have stout rhizomes and the flowering stems are followed by huge basal leaves, long-stalked, green above and downy-grey beneath. Stamens and styles are on separate plants.

Damp meadows and roadsides, banks of streams. March — May.

2   Red Dead-nettle   *Lamium purpureum*   Labiatae
A hairy annual, branching from the base, often purple-tinged, with coarsely-toothed, stalked leaves that are rounded or heart-shaped. The pinkish purple flowers are in close whorls set in the axils of the leaf-like bracts. The tube is longer than the calyx which has short, narrow, pointed teeth.

A common plant in gardens, on cultivated ground and waste land. March — October.

3   Henbit   *Lamium amplexicaule*   Labiatae
An annual with ascending and spreading stems which branch from the base, and with few and rather distant flower-whorls, composed of a pair of stalkless, blunt-toothed bracts, surrounding the flower clusters like a frill. The flowers are rosy-purple, sometimes quite showy but often very small, and have long white hairs on the calyx. Both forms are illustrated. They are in four, close-packed clusters, two to each bract; this shows clearly from below. The lower leaves are small, rounded and blunt-toothed, with long stalks.

Cultivated ground on light, dry soils, common. April — August.

1.

2.

3.

PLATE 49

1   Hedge Woundwort   *Stachys sylvatica*   **Labiatae**
The flowers are in whorls in a loose open spike at the end of the tall stem, which is often branched. They are narrow and two-lipped, wine-red, and the long lower sip is intricately marked with white. The calyx is persistent and short, with five pointed teeth, and encloses four round nutlets, black when ripe. The leaves are large and hairy, heart-shaped at the base, in pairs on the stem below the whorls of flowers; all are stalked. The stem is rough and hairy, square in section and purplish at the angles. The plant has an unpleasant smell when handled.

Woods and shady banks. June − October.

2   Marsh Woundwort   *Stachys palustris*   **Labiatae**
The plant is green, stiff and hairy, with a long creeping rhizome producing small tubers at the apex in autumn. The stem is hollow and not usually branched. The flowers are pale pink with red markings and a broad lower lip, and are in whorls of about six, forming a dense spike at the top of the stem, more spaced out below. The leaves are lanceolate, toothed, and either without or with very short stalks.

Swamps, by streams and ditches. July − September.

3   Common Hemp-nettle   *Galeopsis tetrahit* **agg. Labiatae**
A hairy, branching annual with stems swelling at the nodes. It has the typical hooded flowers of this family, and is very variable in colour, usually pink, sometimes purple or white, with darker markings on the broad lower lip. The leaves are broadly lance-shaped, toothed and stalked. The stem is ridged and has red or yellow glandular hairs.

Widespread and common in fields, and also less often in woods, fens and wet heaths. July − September.

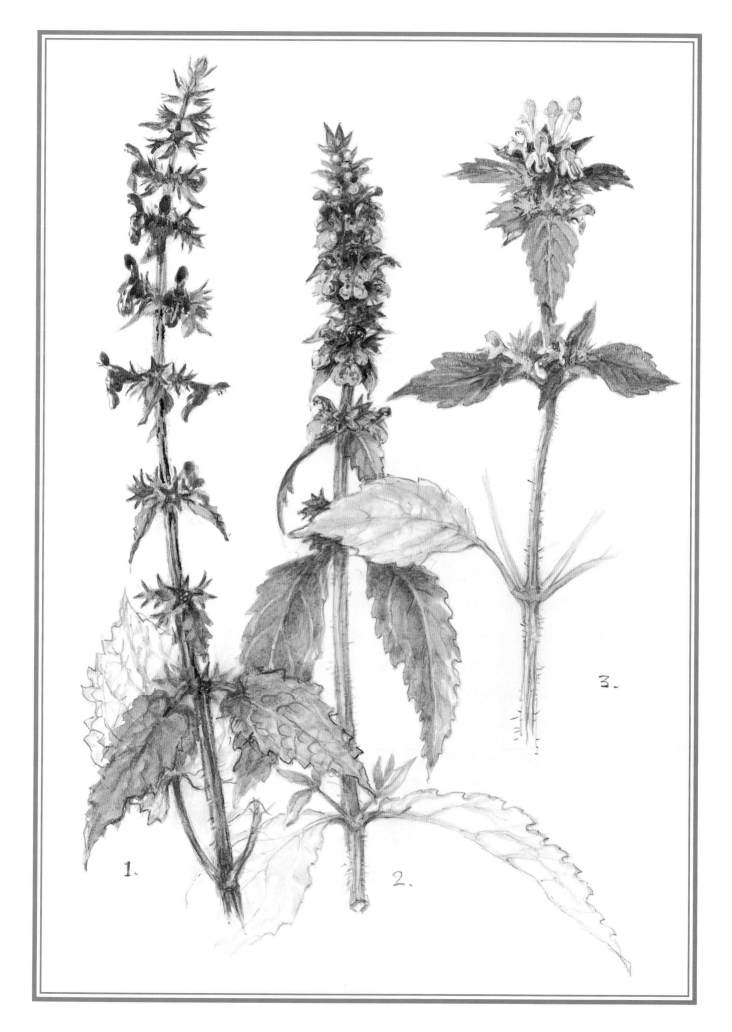

1.

2.

3.

PLATE 50

1   Sea Rocket   *Cakile maritima*   **Cruciferae**

Succulent, smooth and branching, with comparatively large lilac flowers which are followed by oval pods. The leaves are long and pinnately lobed.

An annual plant of sandy coasts. June — September.

2   Coral-wort   *Cardamine bulbifera*   **syn.** *Dentaria bulbifera*   **Cruciferae**

The flowers, like those of the Lady's Smock, are in a cluster at the top of a leaf stem, but they are deeper in colour and are not veined. The uppermost leaves are simple; those lower down are short-stalked and pinnate with a terminal leaflet, and the upper leaves have brown axillary bulbils. The plant, which is perennial, has a creeping whitish rhizome with triangular fleshy scales.

It is very local, mainly in the south. Woods, shady banks, generally on calcareous soil. April — June.

3   Lady's Smock, Cuckoo Flower   *Cardamine pratensis*   **Cruciferae**

The silvery-lilac flowers with their four delicately veined petals and yellow anthers, are in a cluster at the head of the leafy stem, with smaller clusters often rising from the axils of the stem leaves. These stem leaves are alternate and pinnate with very narrow leaflets, but the basal leaves have rounded leaflets and form a rosette.

Damp meadows. April — June.

1.

2.

3.

PLATE 51

1   Red Campion   *Silene dioica*   **Caryophyllaceae**
The large, bright rose-pink flowers have five petals which are very deeply notched; the rounded tubular calyx is ribbed, hairy, often reddish, narrowing into five small teeth. They are in short-stalked clusters branching at the head of tall stems. The upper leaves are sessile, oval and pointed, in opposite pairs; the basal leaves have long winged stalks. The whole plant is covered with silvery hairs.

Shady places and damp ground, woods. May – June.

2   Ragged Robin   *Lychnis flos-cuculi*   **Caryophyllaceae**
The petals of the rose-pink flowers are deeply cut into four very narrow lobes, giving them their characteristically ragged appearance. The tubular calyx is ribbed and dark red. The flowers have slender stalks and grow in loose clusters at the forked ends of the long, erect, downy stems. The stem leaves are stalkless, very narrow, and in widely spaced pairs, those at the base are stalked.

Marshy ground, fens, wet woods and damp meadows. May – June.

PLATE 52

1   Soapwort, Bouncing Bett   *Saponaria officinalis*   **Caryophyllaceae**

Possibly native but probably an early introduction. Wide-spreading with long stout stems that lie on the ground, from which the flowering shoots rise, with pale pink flowers in a branching cluster. The sepals are joined into a long tube with four or five small teeth, and there are usually only two styles. The leaves are broadly lanceolate and pointed with from three to five veins. The plant gets its name from its use in former times for washing. It is still used for delicate embroideries, laces, fine linen, etc.

Hedge-banks, waysides, often near villages, probably an escape from gardens. July — September.

2   Maiden Pink   *Dianthus deltoides*   **Caryophyllaceae**

A low tufted plant with short creeping non-flowering shoots, and ascending flowering shoots, both with narrow pointed grey-green leaves which have hairy edges. The flowers are usually solitary, with long tubular calyx and short pointed epicalyx. The slightly toothed petals are rose-pink, sometimes white, with small spots and a dark basal band.

Rather local, dry sandy fields, dunes, in the south. June — September.

3   Sand or Striated Catchfly   *Silene conica*   **Caryophyllaceae**

Annual. Short, erect, sticky and hairy, with narrow lance-shaped grey-green leaves, and small, bright rose flowers, few in number, with a densely glandular-hairy toothed and swollen calyx.

A local plant of dunes, sandy pastures, along the coasts of south and east Scotland, as far north as Angus. May — June.

4   Night-flowering Campion   *Silene noctiflora*   **Caryophyllaceae**

Annual. A simple or branching plant with softly hairy stems. The basal leaves are oval and stalked, the stem leaves unstalked and narrow and pointed. The petals are deeply cleft, yellowish beneath and rosy above, rolled inwards during the day and open and scented at night.

Rather local on arable fields especially on sandy soils. In the south but as far north as Aberdeen. July — September.

5   Moss Campion   *Silene acaulis*   **Caryophyllaceae**

The bright green moss-like cushion is formed by the densely tufted rosettes of small leaves, and is spangled with the little pink flowers, at first short-stalked but later lengthening. Male and female flowers are on separate plants.

Mountain cliffs, ledges and screes, also on rocks at low levels in the Hebrides, Orkneys and Shetlands. July — August.

1.

2.

3.

4.

5.

PLATE 53

1   Sea Bindweed   *Calystegia soldanella*   Convolvulaceae
Perennial. The rather short stems do not twine like the other species, but are creeping, with shiny, fleshy, kidney-shaped leaves. The solitary flowers are quite large and are pink with white stripes. Sandy and shingly sea-shores, where it spreads by slender, far-creeping rhizomes. It is local in the south-west, and it grows on Eriskay, where it is called 'The Prince's Flower' as it is said to have been introduced by Bonnie Prince Charlie.

June – August.

2   Greater Sand-spurrey   *Spergularia media*   Caryophyllaceae
An almost hairless perennial whose creeping and ascending, flattened shoots rise from a stout stock. The leaves are fleshy, narrow and pointed with horny tips. The starry five-petalled flowers are usually pink or pinkish-white with the short blunt sepals showing and with a centre of ten stamens. The seeds are round with a clear winged border.

Salt marshes round the coast. June – September.

3   Lesser Sand-spurrey   *Spergularia marina*   Caryophyllaceae
This annual is smaller than *S. media* but also has many prostrate shoots. The narrow leaves are flat above and rounded beneath. The petals are deep rose with a white base and are shorter than the blunt, often pink-tinged sepals. The seeds lack a winged border.

Drier parts of the salt marshes. June – September.

4   Cliff Sand-spurrey   *Spergularia rupicola*   Caryophyllaceae
This has a woody stock, with many trailing shoots, often dark purple, and densely hairy and sticky throughout. The leaves are narrow and fleshy with the horny tip prolonged into a sharp point; the stipules are silvery. The petals are deep pink, about the same length as the blunt, white-margined sepals.

Maritime cliffs and rocks, chiefly in the south and west, reaching the Outer Hebrides. June – September.

5   Thrift, Sea-pink   *Armeria maritima*   Plumbaginaceae
The little plant whose bright pink flowers come at once to our minds when we think of the sea-side. It grows in quantity all round our coasts, on rocks, cliffs and salt marshes, and is also found inland on high mountain ledges. The narrow leaves are in cushion-forming rosettes rising from a woody rootstock. The rounded flower-head is at the end of a long stem, enclosed by a cluster of papery-edged bracts which forms a brown tubular sheath round the stem. The five-lobed flowers have a five-pointed, funnel-shaped calyx.

March – November.

1.

2.

3.

4.

5.

PLATE 54

1   Lesser Twayblade   *Listera cordata*   Orchidaceae
A small slender perennial whose stem rises from two brown basal sheaths. Below the middle of the stem there is a pair of opposite, stemless, broadly oval leaves, shining green above and paler below, with a rounded horny tip. The flowers are in a short raceme of about six to twelve, and are reddish tinted with green. The long lip is reddish, hanging down and divided into two narrow diverging segments.

Mountain pine woods and peaty moors, especially among sphagnum. July — September.

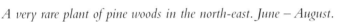

2   Twinflower   *Linnaea borealis*   Caprifoliaceae
A tiny creeping under-shrub, whose prostrate rooting stems can form large mats. The evergreen leaves are rounded, slightly notched at the tips and taper into a short stalk. The slender flower-stems are erect with two delicate, pink, bell-shaped flowers hanging, each on a short stalk, at the top. The flowers are marked with deep pink within, and have two small lance-shaped bracts at the base.

A very rare plant of pine woods in the north-east. June — August.

3   Bog Pimpernel   *Anagallis tenella*   Primulaceae
A tiny slender creeping plant with smooth branching stems that root at the nodes. The little oval leaves are in pairs. The solitary flowers, on long thread-like stalks, rise from the axils of the leaves. They are funnel-shaped with five petals, and are pinkish, or actually white, but with so many fine crimson veins as to appear pink.

Boggy ground near the coast. Mostly in the west, but rare and local. June — August.

4   Scarlet Pimpernel   *Anagallis arvensis* ssp. *arvensis*   Primulaceae
Annual. The spreading, rather prostrate, square stems have opposite pairs of pointed, oval, stalkless leaves which are spotted beneath with black glands. The flowers are solitary, on slender stalks from the leaf axils, and are star-shaped and light red. The petals are fringed with tiny hairs, and are only slightly longer than the sepals.

Cultivated land, dunes. June — August.

5   Sea Milkwort   *Glaux maritima*   Primulaceae
A small perennial with creeping stems which have oval, blunt, fleshy leaves and small pink or white flowers. These are solitary in the leaf axils, stalkless, with a five-lobed calyx, no petals, and five red-stalked stamens.

Common on coasts, in rock crevices and on grassy salt marshes. June — August.

1.

2.

3.

5.

4.

PLATE 55

1 Fragrant Orchid *Gymnadenia conopsea* **Orchidaceae**
The small rosy-lilac flowers are unspotted, and are in a long narrow spike. The two side sepals slope downwards and the lip is broad with three rounded lobes, so that the flower is roughly triangular in shape. The spur is very long and slender. The leaves are long and narrow, unspotted, the upper ones sheathing the stem. It is very sweetly scented, the scent becoming stronger in the evening and lasting through the night.

Grassy places, fens and marshes, usually on base-rich soil. June – August.

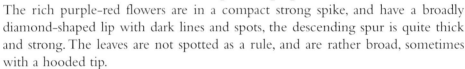

2 Northern Marsh Orchid *Dactylorhiza purpurella* **Orchidaceae**
The rich purple-red flowers are in a compact strong spike, and have a broadly diamond-shaped lip with dark lines and spots, the descending spur is quite thick and strong. The leaves are not spotted as a rule, and are rather broad, sometimes with a hooded tip.

Marshes, fens and damp pastures, usually on base-rich soil. June – July.

3 Heath Spotted Orchid *Dactylorhiza maculata* **ssp. *ericetorum*** **Orchidaceae**
The variable flowers are pale pink or whitish, marked with numerous reddish lines and dots and with a broad lip, three-lobed with the central lobe much smaller than the two widely rounded side lobes and pointed. The leaves are narrow and usually spotted. The spur is slender. Two variations illustrated.

Moist and peaty soils. June – August.

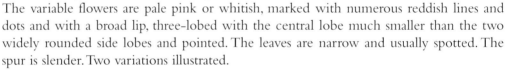

4 Early Purple Orchid *Orchis mascula* **Orchidaceae**
The flowers are rich reddish-purple in a rather lax spike. The lip is about as broad as long, three-lobed, with the central lobe slightly larger and notched. The long spur is stout and blunt, usually pointing upwards. The leaves are rather broad and blunt, but are variable, commonly marked with rounded black-purple spots. It is distinguished from the Northern Marsh Orchid by the membranous flower bracts and the ascending flower spur.

Woods, copses, open pastures, on base-rich soils. April – June.

PLATE 56

1   Marsh Helleborine   *Epipactis palustris*   Orchidaceae

The rhizome is long and creeping with stolon-like branches. The stem is tall, erect, slender and wiry, slightly hairy above and often purplish below with one or two sheathing basal scales. The leaves, four to eight, are oblong-ovate to lanceolate, concave above and often purple beneath; the upper narrow and more erect; all are folded and have prominent veins. The wide-open, drooping flowers are in an open raceme with narrow bracts, and the outer perianth segments are brownish-red and hairy outside. The lip is prominent, broad, white and frilled or curled on the lower part, with yellow spots at the base.

Fens, dune-slacks or sandy ground; local, north to Perth. June — August.

2   Dark Red Helleborine   *Epipactis atrorubens*   Orchidaceae

The rhizome is short, with many long slender roots. The stem is erect, densely but softly hairy, turning violet below. The leaves are elliptical and pointed, narrower above and half-clasping. The wine-red flowers are in a long, open inflorescence, short-stalked, with small pointed bracts, and are faintly fragrant.

Limestone rocks and screes, in woods or in the open, very rare. June — July.

3   Broad-leaved Helleborine   *Epipactis helleborine*   Orchidaceae

The rhizome is usually very short, with numerous roots rising in a cluster from the base of the stem. The stems, one to three, are tall, erect, solid and whitish, with short hairs above, often violet-tinged below, and with two or more basal sheathing scales. The largest leaves are broadly oval and are on the middle of the stem, the upper ones being smaller and narrower; all are strongly veined and dull green. Numerous wide-open, drooping flowers are in a dense raceme. The colours are very variable, different combinations of green, red, pink and purple, often according to whether in shade or in sun.

Woods, wood-margins, hedge-banks. Widespread, but not in the extreme north-east. July — October.

1.

1.

2.

3.

1.

2.

PLATE 57

1   Purple Saxifrage   *Saxifraga oppositifolia*   Saxifragaceae
The large bright rosy flowers are solitary on leafy stems. The small, densely packed, somewhat fleshy, dark green leaves are in opposite pairs though this is not always apparent. Each leaf has a minute lime-secreting pit. When in flower it makes brilliant patches along burn-sides and among damp rocks on mountain sides.

Low and creeping. March — May.

2   Hairy Stonecrop   *Sedum villosum*   Crassulaceae
A small, softly hairy plant with erect reddish stems bearing at the top a loosely branching head of pale pink, five-petalled, starry flowers. The leaves, rounded and succulent, are set alternately along the stem.

Burnsides and wet stony ground on mountains. June — July.

3   Orpine, Livelong   *Sedum telephium*   Crassulaceae
The stems are erect, reddish and smooth, bearing oval leaves which are smooth, fleshy and unstalked, with slightly lobed edges. The flowers are pinkish-lilac with a crimson line down the centre of each petal, and are closely grouped at the head of the stem. It was an old 'healing herb' and besides growing in woods and hedgebanks, it is often found by old garden walls and ruined cottages. The outer skin of the leaf was peeled off and the exposed inner surface was applied to the cut or wound.

July — September.

4   Marsh Rosemary   *Andromeda polifolia*   Ericaceae
A low, hairless, evergreen shrub with creeping rhizomes and scattered erect stems. The leaves are linear, dark green above and bluish-green beneath, with the edges rolled backward. The long-stalked pink flowers, at the ends of the stems, are globular to urn-shaped. The fruit is a rounded dry capsule.

Bogs, as far north as Perth and the Inner Hebrides. April — September.

5   Mountain Azalea   *Loiseleuria procumbens*   Ericaceae
A small, evergreen shrub, intricately branched and mat-forming. The tiny, dark green leaves, oval and shiny, have rolled-under edges, and are set closely along the stem in opposite pairs. The pink flowers are funnel-shaped, opening wide to make bright patches of colour on mountain tops and high moors.

May — July

1.

2.

3.

4.

5.

PLATE 58

1   Heather, Ling   *Calluna vulgaris*   Ericaceae

The well-known heather of the Scottish hills varies in colour from lilac and purple to deep crimson and also, occasionally, white. The tiny flowers are in long leafy spikes; the leaves being very short, narrow and evergreen. The stems are tough and woody, especially in old bushes.

Heaths and moors. August — September.

2   Bell Heather   *Erica cinerea*   Ericaceae

The bells are bright deep red-purple, often in long spikes, and the leaves are tiny, hairless, and dark green, arranged in whorls of three along the stems. These are woody and branching.

It grows on the drier heaths and moors where it makes stretches of brilliant colour.
June — September.

3   Cross-leaved Heath   *Erica tetralix*   Ericaceae

The flowers are a delicate rosy-pink, paler on the underside, and are grouped in compact rounded heads at the ends of the stems. The sparsely hairy leaves are in whorls of four, smaller and more widely spaced near the flower-head, and the whole plant has a greyish appearance.

Damp heaths. July — September.

PLATE 59

1   Cowberry   *Vaccinium vitis-idaea*   Ericaceae
Low-growing and evergreen, with dark green, glossy leaves which are leathery, paler beneath, with in-rolled edges. The flowers are pink, bell-shaped, and in clusters. The fruit is a bright red berry, edible and often gathered for jam-making. It is commonly, though mistakenly, called Cranberry.

Rocky moors, open woods and hillsides, and on acid soils. May – July.

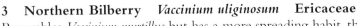

2   Blaeberry, Bilberry   *Vaccinium myrtillus*   Ericaceae
Bushy and erect in habit, with bright green, oval, finely toothed, deciduous leaves on green, angled stems. The flowers are pink or greenish pink, globular, with very short reflexed lobes. The fruit is round and black with a waxy blue bloom and is edible.

Heaths, moors, open woods on acid soil. May – June.

3   Northern Bilberry   *Vaccinium uliginosum*   Ericaceae
Resembles *Vaccinium myrtillus* but has a more spreading habit, the stems brown and rounded, the leaves oval to obtuse and untoothed, blue-green above, whitish and conspicuously netted beneath. The flowers are more oval and the calyx has short lobes.

Mountains and high moors, mostly in the north. April – June.

4   Crowberry   *Empetrum nigrum*   Empetraceae
A prostrate shrub with dense, narrow, evergreen leaves very like those of the heaths, set alternately along the stems which form a close mat. The flowers are very tiny, almost hidden under the leaves, and are pink with six petals. They are dioecious (male and female on different plants). The fruit is an edible round black shiny berry, watery and tasteless.

Moors. At higher altitudes this is usually replaced by Empetrum hermaphroditum, *which is very similar, but the stems are not prostrate, and the flowers are hermaphrodite, often with persistent stamens remaining round the fruit. May – June.*

5   Cranberry   *Vaccinium oxycoccos*   Ericaceae
This slender, creeping evergreen shrubby plant is difficult to find, as it is often partly hidden in the surrounding sphagnum moss. The leaves are oval with the margins rolled downwards, dark green, and whitish beneath. The stems are prostrate and rooting, usually widely separated from each other. The flowers are distinctive, they are small, pink, with lobes that turn back exposing the prominent stamens, like tiny cyclamen. The fruit is a rounded berry, sometimes more pear-shaped, red but often with brownish markings.

Wet, boggy hillsides. June – August.

6   Bearberry   *Arctostaphylos uva-ursi*   Ericaceae
A prostrate, mat-forming and wide-spreading, evergreen shrub with dark green, oval leaves which are paler and veined beneath; they are untoothed and leathery. The flowers are rounded, whitish, constricted and pink at the mouth, and in short, close clusters. The fruit is a red shiny berry.

It is a widespread, common plant of mountain moors or open woods on acid soils.
May – July.

PLATE 60

1   Common Centaury   *Centaurium erythraea*   Gentianaceae
A hairless annual with a basal rosette of rather oval leaves that are prominently three to seven-veined, the stem leaves being shorter and narrower. The pink star-shaped flowers are usually stalkless and are closely clustered in a branched inflorescence. The stamens on each flower arise from the top of the corolla tube.

Dry grassland, woods margins. Mostly south but reaching Moray and the Outer Hebrides. June – October.

2   Purple Loosestrife   *Lythrum salicaria*   Lythraceae
This downy, erect perennial produces a spike-like inflorescence of rosy-purple, narrow-petalled flowers, arranged in whorls in axils of bracts. The stalkless leaves are oval-lanceolate and pointed, in open pairs or in whorls of three lower down.

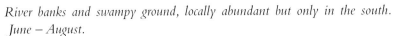

River banks and swampy ground, locally abundant but only in the south. June – August.

3   Pink Purslane   *Claytonia sibirica* syn. *Montia sibirica*   Portalucaceae
The rather fleshy, long-stalked, shiny, green, basal leaves are oval and distinctly veined. The two stem leaves are stalkless and opposite but not joined, and surround the flowering stalks which carry several flowers whose five notched petals are pink with darker veins. This is a North American plant, but it has become widely naturalised and forms large beds in damp woods and shaded streamsides, especially in the west and north.

April – July.

1.

2.

3.

PLATE 61

1   Rose-bay Willow-herb   *Epilobium angustifolium*   syn. *Chamaenerion angustifolium*
Onagraceae

Extremely invasive, this tall plant with its spikes of aggressive bright rose-purple flowers, now dominates much of the countryside, spreading rapidly where there are wood clearings, wood-margins, disturbed ground, and even in gardens, both by its long creeping roots and by innumerable wind-blown seeds. The lance-shaped leaves are arranged spirally and closely along the strong erect stems. The four petals are irregularly grouped with the long, stalk-like seed-pod behind them which thickens and lengthens and splits when ripe, releasing the seeds with their long silky hairs.

July — September.

2   Great Hairy Willow-herb, Codlins and Cream   *Epilobium hirsutum*   **Onagraceae**

A tall, perennial, very leafy plant with erect round downy stems, and white fleshy underground stolons produced in summer. The upper leaves are lance-shaped, in opposite pairs, and clasp the stem. The four-petalled flowers are bright purplish-rose, the buds erect. The stigma has four prominent creamy lobes that arch back.

Fens, marshes, banks of streams. July — August.

3   Broad-leaved Willow-herb   *Epilobium montanum*   **Onagraceae**

This is a very common garden weed, whose small, pale rose flowers with their four notched petals and the long seed-pods which quickly follow are familiar sights. The leaves are in pairs and the stems are often reddish.

June — September.

PLATE 62

1   Lousewort   *Pedicularis sylvatica*   **Scrophulariaceae**
A low-growing perennial with prostrate branches from the base. The small pinnate leaves have toothed lobes The pink flowers are comparatively large, with a long hooded upper lip which has a single tooth on each side near the tip. The rather inflated calyx, usually glabrous, divides at the mouth into five leaf-like lobes.

Damp heaths, moors and bogs. April — July.

2   Marsh Lousewort, Red Rattle   *Pedicularis palustris*   **Scrophulariaceae**
Resembling *P. sylvatica* but an annual or biennial with a single erect, branched reddish stem. The leaves are pinnatifid, deeply cut, with toothed lobes. The purplish-pink flowers have a darker upper lip, arching forward, with a tooth at each side near the tip and another further down; the lower lip is wide and three-lobed The inflated calyx is ribbed and hairy with two short leaf-like lobes at the mouth.

Bogs and wet heaths. May — September.

3   Red Bartsia   *Odontites vernus*   **Scrophulariaceae**
A downy, purple-tinted annual, slender, erect and branching, with unstalked leaves which are broadly lance-shaped and sparsely toothed. The flowers which rise from the axils of the leaf-like bracts are pink and two-lipped, the upper lip hooded and the lower three-lobed. The calyx is bell-shaped, hairy and four-toothed.

Cultivated fields and waste ground. June — July.

1.

2.

3.

PLATE 63

1   Valerian   *Valeriana officinalis*   Valerianaceae

A tall, erect perennial plant with grooved stems which are hairy below, with terminal, branched clusters of pale pink flowers; these are tubular, five-lobed, with three stamens, and are pouched at the base. The leaves are opposite, pinnate, small and sharply pointed above, and much larger further down where they are stalked and have long, broadly lanceolate, toothed leaflets. The fruit is oblong, with a parachute of white, feathery pappus.

Grassy and bushy places, both in dry and damp areas. June – August.

2   Foxglove   *Digitalis purpurea*   Scrophulariaceae

A tall, handsome plant, usually biennial, whose leaves form a rosette the first year, followed the second year by the tall erect spike of large rosy-purple bells, hanging from one side of the stem. They have deeper purple spots on white patches inside the flower, conspicuous on the long lower lobe. The calyx is much shorter than the corolla; it is cup-like with pointed lobes. the basal leaves are very large, oval, softly downy, green above and densely grey-haired beneath, and bluntly toothed. They are wrinkled and the network of veins stands out in sharp relief below. The whole plant is poisonous.

The drug, digitalin, is obtained from the leaves. It is one of the handsomest of our native wild flowers.

Open woods, roadsides, often appearing in large numbers where woods have been felled.
June – September.

1.

2.

PLATE 64

1   Common Fumitory   *Fumaria officinalis*   **Fumariaceae**
A common annual weed of fields and gardens. The narrow pink short-stalked flowers which are tube-like, with the petals joined up to the blackish-red tips, are in loose spikes at the ends of long stems. The leaves are much divided and fern-like, with small flat lobes. There are a number of similar species which are not easily distinguished.

May — October.

2   Figwort   *Scrophularia nodosa*   **Scrophulariaceae**
An erect perennial of medium height with a short rhizome and square stems which have pairs of pointed, short-stalked, coarsely-toothed leaves. The flowers are in a loose inflorescence and have two dark red-brown upper lobes, three green lower ones, and four fertile stamens. The plant has a strong sharp smell.

Damp woods and hedge-banks. June — September.

3   Hound's-tongue   *Cynoglossum officinale*   **Boraginaceae**
An erect greyish-downy biennial of medium height which smells of mice. The leaves are long, entire, with wavy margins and very hairy on both surfaces. The lower ones are stalked, the upper sessile. The flowers are usually dull red-purple, but sometimes white, with five blunt sepals. The fruits are covered with hooked bristles.

Grassy places, borders of woods on dry soils, particularly near the sea. Rather local but north to Angus. June — August.

1.

2 -

3.

PLATE 65

**1   Common Persicaria, Redshank   *Persicaria maculosa* syn. *Polygonum persicaria*
Polygonaceae**

An annual with tiny pinkish flowers which are set tightly in a close-packed spike of buds, with individual flowers only opening at intervals. The smooth, reddish stems, swollen at the nodes with papery, fringed sheathing stipules, are branching and spreading, erect or lying on the ground. The smooth leaves are lance-shaped, narrowing at the base and often black blotched.

Common on cornfields, cultivated and waste ground. June — October.

2   Bistort, Snake-root   *Persicaria bistorta* syn. *Polygonum bistorta*   Polygonaceae

The small, pale pink flowers are in a dense spike at the end of a tall smooth unbranched stem. The stem leaves are narrowly triangular with blunt sheathing stipules at the base which form a tube round the stem. The basal leaves are long-stalked, with a wing running half-way down the stalk; they are large and broad, tapering to a pointed tip and often blotched with brown spots. The rhizome is very stout and contorted.

Meadows and grassy roadsides, often forming large patches. June — August.

3   Knotgrass   *Polygonum aviculare*   Polygonaceae

A spreading, glabrous, mostly prostrate annual. The narrow, lance-shaped leaves are set at intervals along the smooth stems and at the base of each there is a close cluster of about two to four small pink and white flowers, partly enclosed in a silvery membrane or ochraea.

Waste ground, arable land and sea shore. July — October.

4 Amphibious Bistort *Persicaria amphibia* syn. *Polygonum amphibium* Polygonaceae

There are two forms. One is found floating in slow-moving water, and is hairless, and the stems root at the nodes while the leaves are cordate or heart-shaped at the base. The second form is hairy, the stems erect and only rooting at the lower nodes, the leaves rounded at the base; this form grows at the water's edge. Both have dense terminal flower-heads of small pink or red flowers.

July — September.

PLATE 66

1 Whin, Gorse *Ulex europaeus* **Leguminosae**

An evergreen shrub where the leaves have become long, rigid, grooved spines, set at the ends of the short branches which also bear the rich, golden-yellow flowers with their coconut scent. The calyx is thin and yellow, covered with fine hairs, and is in two halves. Young seedling plants have soft hairy leaves, but they gradually turn into sharp spines, so that the whole bush becomes densely prickly. Sheep often browse on the soft young shoots, giving the bushes a rounded neatly-pruned appearance. In earlier times whin was used for fodder, being bruised to a nutritious pulp by stone 'whin-mills', still occasionally found, derelict, on old farms.

Common on roadsides, heaths and waste ground. From March throughout most of the year. 'Ye canna kiss the lassies when the whin is nae in flower.'

2 Broom *Cytisus scoparius* **syn.** *Sarothamnus scoparius* **Leguminosae**

A tall branching deciduous shrub with small clover-like leaves set all along the ridged stems. The flowers are slightly paler than those of the whin. They are a little larger, and have short stalks. The seed-pods are long and black, and explode to scatter the seed.

Common on dry heaths and moors and by roadsides. April – June.

3 Petty Whin *Genista anglica* **Leguminosae**

A small scrambling under-shrub, its stems set with sharp spines. The little yellow pea-flowers are axillary towards the ends of the branches and the leaves are small, narrow and pointed.

Heaths and moors, often amongst heather. April – June.

PLATE 67

1   Meadow Vetchling   *Lathyrus pratensis*   Leguminosae
The bright yellow flowers, with their tiny stalks, are in a close cluster at the end of a long slender stem. The leaves have two lance-shaped leaflets usually ending in a single tendril, and there are two arrow-shaped stipules where the short leaf-stalk joins the main stem, which is branching and climbing. Perennial.

Hedges, grassy places, waysides. May – August.

2   Bird's-foot Trefoil   *Lotus corniculatus*   Leguminosae
The yellow flowers are often streaked with red, and are in a circular flat head of about three to eight on a long stem. The leaves have five leaflets, the end three appearing as if trifoliate, the lower pair close to the main stem. The seed pods are brown, pointed, spreading like the claws of a bird's foot. It is a spreading, variable and common perennial plant of waysides, field and meadows.

May – September.

3   Large Bird's-foot Trefoil   *Lotus pedunculatus* syn. *Lotus uliginosus*   Leguminosae
This resembles the Bird's-foot trefoil but is larger, more erect and branching, and the leaflets are much broader. It scrambles up through the herbage of damp waysides, woods and marshes.

June – September.

1.

2.

3.

PLATE 68

1   Hop Trefoil   *Trifolium campestre*   **Leguminosae**
The closely packed heads of yellow flowers are set at the end of a short stalk rising from the axil of a trifoliate leaf, which has a much shorter stalk and no point. The flowers have a broad standard which turns brown as it fades. There are tiny erect stipules at the junction of leaves and stems. It is an annual of rather erect habit, growing in grassy places and waste ground.

June — September.

2   Lesser Yellow Trefoil   *Trifolium dubium*   **Leguminosae**
A small, prostrate and spreading annual. The tiny yellow clustered flower head rises on a short stalk from the axil of the trifoliate leaf or leaves. The standard is narrow, folding over the fruit, and turns brown as it fades.

Grassy places and waysides. May — October.

3   Kidney Vetch, Ladies' Fingers   *Anthyllis vulneraria*   **Leguminosae**
Usually erect, the whole plant is covered with silky hairs. The rounded flower-heads are in a close pair, the individual flowers embedded in a woolly calyx, and the whole flower-head is half encircled at the base by two sharply dissected leafy bracts. The leaves are pinnate, those on the stem having narrow pointed leaflets, those at the base one large end leaflet with two or more pairs of smaller leaflets below. The flowers are usually yellow, sometimes reddish or white.

Dry places, screes, shallow soils. June — September.

1.

3.

2.

PLATE 69

1   Milk-vetch, Wild Liquorice   *Astragalus glycyphyllos*   Leguminosae
A tall, sturdy perennial with strong smooth stems which zigzag and bear a pinnate leaf at each angle. There is a short-stemmed inflorescence stalk in the leaf axil, which has a sheathing stipule. The flowers are cream, tinged with green.

Calcareous grass-land and scrub, local. July — August.

2   Dyer's Greenweed   *Genista tinctoria*   Leguminosae
A small erect shrub with slender brown branching stems, green young twigs and no spines. The leaves are lance-shaped, fringed with hairs and almost stalkless. The yellow flowers are in close terminal racemes, with standard equalling keel. The pods are flat, tapering but blunt at both ends, and hairless.

Rough pastures, scrub. Only in the south and not common. July — September.

3   Yellow Oxytropis   *Oxytropis campestris*   Leguminosae
This resembles Purple Oxytropis with silky-hairy leaflets and a pointed keel to the pod. The flowers are pale yellow tinged with purple. The inflorescence stalk is shorter than the leaf at flowering but lengthens later.

A very rare plant of rocky mountain ledges. June — July.

1.

2.

3.

PLATE 70

1   Cowslip   *Primula veris*   **Primulaceae**
The flowers are cup-shaped, deep yellow with an orange spot at the base of each petal; the flower-tube long and partly sheathed by the pale green, tubular calyx. They are in a somewhat one-sided, drooping cluster at the end of a long smooth stem, and are sweetly scented. The leaves, like those of the primrose, are wrinkled and toothed, but they narrow abruptly about half-way down and the stalk is then winged.

Fields, open woods, and often on grassy banks by the sea. April — May.

2   False Oxlip   *Primula veris* **x** *Primula vulgaris*   **Primulaceae**
The flowers are a deeper yellow than *P. vulgaris*, and larger and paler than *P. veris*. It is found where primroses and cowslips grow near each other, and is intermediate between the parents, and variable. The flower-cluster is not one-sided as in the true Oxlip, which is a distinct species, *P. elatior*, and does not occur in Scotland.

April — May.

3   Primrose   *Primula vulgaris*   **Primulaceae**
The pale greenish-yellow flowers, solitary on their slender stalks, come early in the spring, and have a delicate scent. The stalks are downy and pinkish, they rise from a rosette of dark green leaves, long, oval and wrinkled, tapering towards the stalk. They have a network of veins which are prominent on the under surface. All grow from a sturdy rhizome which gradually lengthens as the young growth and fresh roots spread from the top.

Woods, grassy banks, sea cliffs. March — May, and occasionally in the autumn.

PLATE 71

1   Yellow Loosestrife   *Lysimachia vulgaris*   **Primulaceae**
The erect downy stems spring from a creeping perennial root-stock, and are leafy, the leaves being either in pairs or in whorls of two to four, and broadly lance-shaped, stalkless, and dotted with tiny black glands. The flowers, at the top of the stem, are in small leafy clusters on short stalks rising from the axils of the leaves, forming a leafy panicle. They are five-petalled, starry, with orange dots in the centre. The petals join to form a small tube, with small pointed sepals which have orange or reddish margins.

Fens, river-banks, damp places. Locally common northwards to Inverness. July — August.

2   Yellow Pimpernel   *Lysimachia nemorum*   **Primulaceae**
The small starry flowers are solitary on thread-like stalks rising from the axils of the leaves which are set in pairs along the smooth, reddish stems. These are spreading and prostrate and root at intervals. The leaves are smooth, oval and pointed, the fruits round.

Woods, shady hedge-banks. May — September.

3   Creeping Jenny   *Lysimachia nummularia*   **Primulaceae**
Mat-forming perennial with long creeping leafy stems that root at the nodes. The leaves are opposite, in pairs with short stalks; they are wide, oval and blunt, smooth and rather shiny. The solitary yellow flowers, also in pairs, rise on short stalks from the leaf axils. They are rather cup-shaped, with the lobes fringed with tiny hairs. The sepals are heart-shaped and pointed. Fruit is rarely, if ever, produced in Britain.

Damp hedge-banks, grassy places. South to central Scotland. June — August.

1.

2.

3.

PLATE 72

1   Yellow Mountain Saxifrage   *Saxifraga aizoides*   Saxifragaceae
The short leafy stems rise erect from a mat of narrow fleshy leaves. The flowers, in a loose head, have five narrow yellow petals, spaced so that the sepals show between, each petal has an orange spot at the base. The golden yellow flowers make bright patches of colour along the sides of mountain streams and on wet rocky places on hillsides.

June — September.

2   Wall-pepper, Stonecrop   *Sedum acre*   Crassulaceae
Evergreen and mat-forming, with small rounded fleshy leaves that are hot and acrid to the taste, and grow closely along the stems in a spiral. The bright yellow star-like flowers are in small branching groups at the heads of the short erect stems.

Sandy places, old walls, rocks. June — July.

3   Roseroot   *Sedum rosea*   syn. *Rhodiola rosea*   Crassulaceae
Smooth and glaucous, the erect stems rise from a thick, fleshy, branching root-stock, which projects above ground level. The small flowers, in a close flat-topped head, have four narrow, greenish-yellow petals and four sepals, male and female flowers on separate plants. The male flower is illustrated, with stamens. The leaves are thick, succulent, glaucous, often rose-tipped growing closely in a spiral along the flower stem, largest at the top, where they form a rosette below the flower-head, and progressively growing smaller down the stem.

Crevices of sea cliffs and mountain rocks.

4   Golden Saxifrage, opposite-leaved   *Chrysosplenium oppositifolium*   Saxifragaceae
There are two distinct forms of this plant. In this one the creeping stems lie on the ground, spreading and rooting with the rounded, short-stalked leaves in opposite pairs. The golden-yellow flowers are very tiny, with three leaf-like bracts in the clusters at the ends of forking stems; they have no petals, and the colour is given by the four rounded sepals and the bright yellow stamens.

Shady, damp places, stream-sides. March — July.

Golden Saxifrage, alternate-leaved   *Chrysosplenium alternifolium*   Saxifragaceae
Here the erect flowering stems rise from underground, creeping stolons, but the stem leaves are alternate, although similarly rounded and blunt-toothed. The stems are triangular, instead of being square. It is a slightly larger plant, with basal leaves long-stalked and kidney-shaped.

It is much more local, in similar wet and damp places, but not in the extreme west. March — June. (not illustrated)

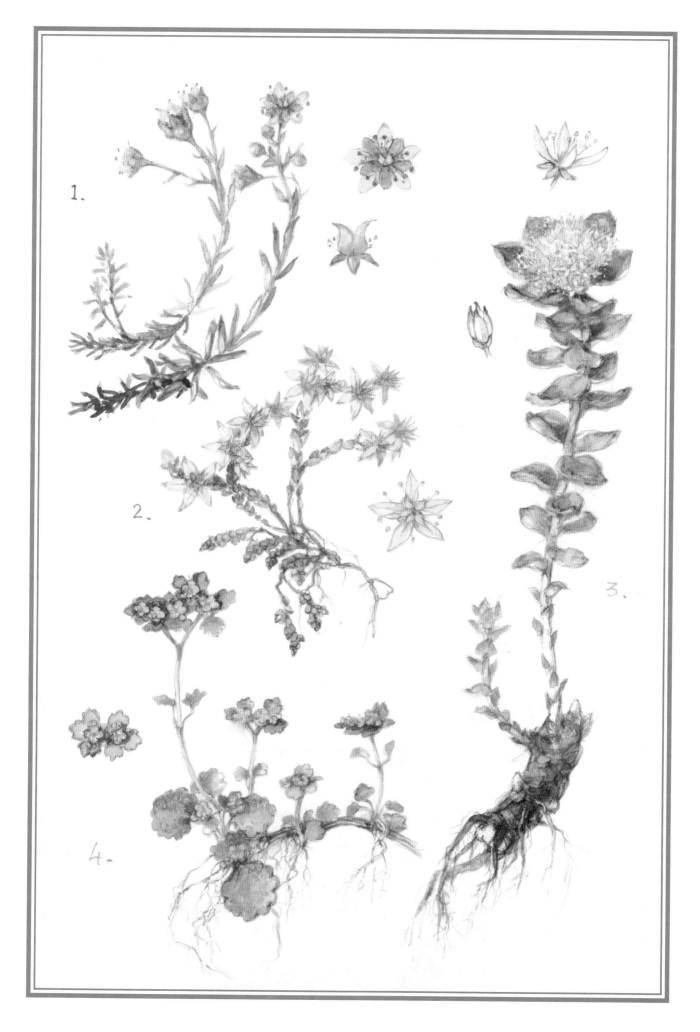

PLATE 73

1   Common St John's Wort   *Hypericum perforatum*   **Hypericaceae**

There are many clusters of five-petalled yellow flowers at the tops of the branching stems, with the numerous stamens joined at the base into three bunches. The stems are smooth and erect with two raised lines and are woody at the base.   The leaves are in pairs, stalkless and having translucent glandular dots.

Open woods, hedgebanks, grassland. Common. June — September.

2   Tutsan   *Hypericum androsaemum*   **Hypericaceae**

A medium tall shrubby plant, half-evergreen, with a woody stock from which rise several long erect flowering stems. The flowers are small, five-petalled, rather dull yellow, and in a flat cluster rising from the axils of two large, leafy bracts. The oval sepals, two small, and three larger, show between the petals. The stamens are numerous and conspicuous, in five bunches slightly joined at the base. The fruit is a berry, red at first, later turning black. The leaves are in pairs, large, broad and egg-shaped (ovate), slightly heart-shaped at the base, smooth and stalkless.

Thickets, woods and hedges, especially in the west. June — August.

3   Trailing St John's Wort   *Hypericum humifusum*   **Hypericaceae**

The slender stems are prostrate and have two raised lines; they are slightly woody at the base. The small starry flowers are rather few, with petals only slightly longer than the sepals, which are unequal. It is an attractive little creeping perennial, often in gardens, and on gravelly banks and heaths.

Acid soil. June — September.

1.

2.

2.

3.

PLATE 74

1   Square-stemmed St John's Wort   *Hypericum tetrapterum*   **Hypericaceae**
A smooth and erect perennial with sturdy square stems that are winged at the angles and reddish. The leaves are oval and stalkless, and become more rounded nearer the foot of the stem. The flowers are small, pale yellow, and are grouped at the top of the stem in rather close clusters.

Damp meadows, marshes. June — September.

2   Slender St John's Wort   *Hypericum pulchrum*   **Hypericaceae**
The stems are erect, slender, sometimes reddish, and smooth. The gland-dotted leaves are in pairs along the stem at intervals. They are small, oval and stalkless, and from their axils rise the flowering stems with three flowers, which have pointed, bright yellow petals tinged with red, and many stamens. The buds are red. The sepals are short and oval and have tiny black glands along the margins; these are also near the margins of the petals but are extremely small. It is a beautiful little plant, well worth a place in the rock garden.

Dry banks, open woods. June — August.

3   Hairy St John's Wort   *Hypericum hirsutum* **Hypericaceae**
Erect, rounded, hairy stems with unstalked, downy broadly oval leaves. The flowers are pale yellow, with pointed sepals which have short-stalked black glands along their margins.

Woods, damp grassy places. July — August.

1.

2.

3.

PLATE 75

1   Rock Rose   *Helianthemum nummularium*   **Cistaceae**
Small, shrubby and rather prostrate, with the flowering branches rising from the woody main stem. The five-petalled flowers are soft and silky, with two very small and three large ribbed sepals, and are in loose clusters with drooping buds. The leaves are lanceolate to oblong, set in pairs along the stem with tiny stipules at their base; they are one-veined and downy-white beneath.

Grassy and rocky places by the sea and on hills. June — September.

2   Tormentil   *Potentilla erecta*   **Rosaceae**
The small flower, solitary and long-stalked, has four petals divided by narrow sepals so that it resembles a Maltese Cross. The branching stems are very slender, decumbent to erect, springing from a thick woody rootstock, spreading widely but never rooting; in this way they differ from the Trailing Tormentil, *Potentilla anglica*. The stem leaves are stalkless or almost so, cut into three narrow toothed leaflets, with two palmately lobed stipules at their base, appearing like extra leaflets, the whole forming a whorl round the stem. The long-stalked basal leaves are in a rosette which often withers and disappears before flowering time. The stem leaves often colour attractively, turning red and yellow.

Very common on moors, acid hillsides and mountains. June — September.

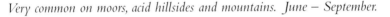

3   Hoary Cinquefoil   *Potentilla argentea*   **Rosaceae**
Rather resembling Tormentil, *Potentilla erecta*, but with five petals, woolly stems, leaves densely silvery below, and with five leaflets but with two small stipules at the base, the lower being stalked but the upper leaves only very shortly stalked.

Dry, sandy grassland, more common in the west. June — September.

4   Silverweed   *Potentilla anserina*   **Rosaceae**
The five-petalled, bright yellow flowers are solitary at the end of long slender stalks rising from a rosette of pinnate leaves, silky and silvery beneath. Also spreading from the basal rosette are the very long, creeping, rooting and flowering stolons. On each leaf the pairs of leaflets, oval and evenly toothed, alternate with smaller ones.

Common on roadsides, dunes, damp and waste ground. June — August.

1.

2.

3.

4.

PLATE 76

1   Wood Avens, Herb Bennet *Geum urbanum* **Rosaceae**

A tall leafy perennial, with the flowers usually borne singly, erect at the head of the stem. They are small, five-petalled, with conspicuous pointed sepals between the petals, and backed by an epicalyx. When the fruit develops the styles persist as reddish, hooked awns which catch in any passing object. The stem leaves are toothed and pinnate with large leaf-like stipules below them, the basal leaves being much larger and broader with two small leaflets between each pair further down the long stalk.

It is a common plant of open woods and shady places; it hybridises with the Water Avens. May – September.

2   Wood Sage *Teucrium scorodonia* **Labiatae**

Perennial. The flowers are in long branching racemes which are small, one-lipped, greenish-yellow, with four prominent red stamens, and are in pairs. The branching, side racemes rise from the axils of the pairs of leaves further down the stem. The leaves are soft, heart-shaped and wrinkled like sage, and are stalked.

Open woods, heaths, fixed dunes. July – September.

2.

1.

PLATE 77

1   Agrimony *Agrimonia eupatoria*   **Rosaceae**
An erect hairy perennial, often with reddish stems. The leaves are pinnate with two or three pairs of smaller leaflets between each pair of the main ones, which are acute and strongly toothed. The flowers are in a long spike and have five yellow petals, five sepals. The fruit is covered with hooked spines. The plant is not fragrant; *A. odorata* is similar but has fragrant leaves, sticky underneath, and grows in similar places in the south.

Hedgebanks, roadsides, field-edges, but rare in the north. Both June — August.

2   Large-flowered Hemp-nettle   *Galeopsis speciosa*   **Labiatae**
This is larger and more robust than the Common Hemp-nettle, and is a handsome annual plant with large pale yellow flowers which have a prominent violet lower lip. The flowers are in whorls along the rough bristly stem, each in a pointed toothed calyx, which is about half as long as the flower-tube. The large oval stalked leaves, hairy and coarsely toothed, are at the base of each whorl of flowers.

Arable land, rather local, often on acid soil. July — September.

3   Annual Woundwort   *Stachys annua*   **Labiatae**
The creamy-yellow flowers are in whorls along the stem. The oval toothed leaves taper towards the stalk.

Not native but very common on cultivated and waste land. June — October.

1.

2.

3.

PLATE 78

1   Lady's Bedstraw   *Galium verum*   Rubiaceae
The small clusters of tiny four-petalled flowers are on short stalks which rise in pairs from a whorl of fine needle-like leaves. These are spaced at intervals along the erect, four-angled, branching stem which has the appearance of a long spike of flowers. The plant has a slender creeping stock and is perennial.

Dry, sandy places, roadside banks, dunes. Very common. July   August.

2   Crosswort   *Galium laevipes* syn. *Galium cruciata*   Rubiaceae
The small, yellow, honey-scented flowers are in dense axillary clusters, rather shorter than the leaves. These are in whorls of four, in the shape of a cross, and are oval, three-veined, yellow-green and hairy.

Open woodland and scrub, hedgerows, waysides. More common in the south. May – June.

3   Yellow Rattle   *Rhinanthus minor*   Scrophulariaceae
The flowers have a conspicuous inflated bladder-like calyx which half encloses the tubular two-lipped corolla. The upper lip is like a hood, with two small teeth, and the lower three-lobed. The flowers are in pairs in the axils of the two broadly linear sharply toothed, unstalked leaves which are spaced at intervals along the stem. The stem is branching, four-angled, and sometimes dark-spotted. When the plant withers, it is an annual, the seeds rattling inside the dry capsules.

Damp   meadows, fens, grassy places on mountains. May – September.

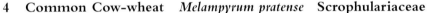

4   Common Cow-wheat   *Melampyrum pratense*   Scrophulariaceae
An annual. The pale yellow flowers are usually at the base of narrow leafy bracts, in pairs both turned to the same side, and are two-lipped, with the lower lip straight, three-lobed and directed forward. The corolla tube is about twice as long as the calyx which has sharply pointed teeth pointing upwards. The leaves are in pairs, long, narrow and almost stalkless. The stem is erect with spreading branches.

Woods and heaths. May – October.

1.

2.

3.

4.

PLATE 79

1   Mimulus, Monkey-flower   *Mimulus guttatus*   Scrophulariaceae
The large showy flowers are two-lipped and lobed, with the throat and upper part of the lower lip marked with small red spots. The three-lobed lower lip is much longer than the upper and the throat is nearly closed by the prominent palate. The oblong toothed leaves are in alternate pairs along the smooth, ridged, usually erect stems. It is perennial and a native of North America but is thoroughly naturalised here and is a common plant of streams and ditches.

July – August.

2   Blood-drop Emlets   *Mimulus luteus*   Scrophulariaceae
The large red spots on the lobes distinguish this from the more common *M. guttatus*. The other distinguishing features are the open throat, the lower lip being only a little longer than the upper, and the usually decumbent flower stems. It grows in similar places. Also perennial, it is not a native. June – September.

The hybrid, Mimulus guttatus x luteus *has a much larger red area than* M. luteus.

3   Bog Asphodel   *Narthecium ossifragum*   Liliaceae
The stiff, smooth, lance-shaped leaves, often curved and usually five-veined, all rise from a creeping rhizome. The stem leaves are few, smaller and sheathing. The deep yellow, starry flowers are in a close raceme at the head of the flowering stem. The stamens have woolly filaments and orange anthers. In fruit the whole plant turns bright orange, bringing vivid colour to the acid bogs, wet heaths and moors where the plant is common and plentiful. It is perennial.

July – August.

1.

2.

3.

PLATE 80

1   Great Mullein, Aaron's Rod   *Verbascum thapsus*   Scrophulariaceae
Biennial. Very tall and conspicuous, to 2 metres, with its high, winged, reddish stem ending in a long dense terminal spike of bright yellow flowers which only open at intervals along the spike. The whole plant is thickly covered with soft whitish wool. The stem leaves are oval and pointed, narrowing into a winged stalk, the large basal leaves stalked with cordate base, and having a reddish midrib. The flowers have very short stalks, five rounded petal lobes, and five stamens, of which the upper three only are clothed thickly with whitish or yellowish hairs. Occasionally there are small side racemes from the axils of the upper leaves.

Sunny banks and waste places usually on a dry soil. June — August.

2   Dark Mullein   *Verbas cum nigrum*   Scrophulariaceae
Biennial. Erect, but not so tall, with a ridged stem, and leaves which are dark green above, pale beneath, and only thinly downy. The upper leaves are stalkless, the large basal leaves having cordate bases and long reddish stalks. The flowers are yellow with rather curled petals, purple-spotted at the base, and all the stamens are thickly clothed with purple hair.   The anthers are bright orange. Like the Great Mullein there are sometimes axillary racemes from the axils of the upper leaves.

Waysides and open banks, but only casual in Scotland. June — September.

PLATE 81

1   Lesser Meadow Rue   *Thalictrum minus*   Ranunculaceae

There are a number of closely related forms, but all have the drooping, tassel, shaped yellow flowers, the wiry branching stems, and the pinnate leaves with rounded, lobed leaflets, rather variable in size but usually as broad as long. The flowers are in loose clusters with four inconspicuous, pale greenish or purplish perianth segments, and long yellow stamens which hang down.

Sand dunes, grassy places, rocks, mountains, sea cliffs. June — August.

2   Yellow Toadflax   *Linaria vulgaris*   Scrophulariaceae

Perennial. The erect stems have numerous long, narrow, smooth leaves, and at the top there is a raceme of flowers. These point upwards, and are yellow with a long spur; in the centre the rounded part, or palate, is deep orange.

Edges of fields, hedge banks and waste ground, mostly in south Scotland. July — October.

1.   2.

PLATE 82

1 Yellow Flag *Iris pseudacorus* **Iridaceae**

The large bright yellow flowers have three broad outer segments, marked near the centre with an orange patch, outlined with thin brown lines; there are three ascending inner segments, and three flattened curved styles which hide the black stamens. The flowers are sheathed by a spathe, and there are about three on a stem, which is tall, stiffly erect and branched. The leaves are long, sword-shaped and erect, with a raised mid-rib. It is a handsome plant, specially beautiful when seen growing in large numbers by river and loch sides, especially in the west.

June – August.

2 Marsh Marigold, Kingcup *Caltha palustris* **Ranunculaceae**

Another waterside plant, with large, bright, golden-yellow flowers, widely cup-shaped, made up of five to six sepals surrounding a boss of golden stamens with greenish carpels at their centre, which will later swell into large pods. The leaves are rounded or heart-shaped, dark green and shiny, the upper leaves clasping the stems while the basal leaves have long stalks. The long thick stems are smooth and hollow, mostly lying on the damp ground, or floating in shallow water.

Marshy places and by burns. March – May.

1.

2 -

PLATE 83

1   Goldilocks *Ranunculus auricomus*   Ranunculaceae
An erect and slightly branching perennial, with smooth stems and very variable leaves, the upper ones are narrow, pointed and stalkless; lower down the stem they become more lobed although still narrow, and the basal leaves have long stalks and are divided into three broad toothed lobes. The rather few golden-yellow flowers have a deformed appearance as the five petals are of different sizes, or some even absent.

Woodlands, damp and shady places. April – May.

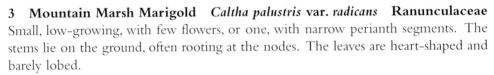

2   Lesser Spearwort   *Ranunculus flammula*   Ranunculaceae
A smooth-stemmed, rather prostrate perennial with ascending flowering stems. The flowers are small, pale yellow and glossy. The leaves are lanceolate, smooth and stalked, and, where they join the stem, sheathed with a whitish membrane; the lower leaves have longer stalks and are larger. The stems lie on the ground and root at intervals at the nodes.

Common on the wet shingly banks of rivers and lochs. June – August.

3   Mountain Marsh Marigold   *Caltha palustris* var. *radicans*   Ranunculaceae
Small, low-growing, with few flowers, or one, with narrow perianth segments. The stems lie on the ground, often rooting at the nodes. The leaves are heart-shaped and barely lobed.

Marshy ground on mountains. April – July.

4   Semi-double Buttercup   *Ranunculus repens* var.   Ranunculaceae
Recently found on a roadside in Strathdon, and probably a sport of *R. repens*, this specimen is semi-double with ten petals arranged in two circles, five outer and five inner. They are sharply pointed, and rounded at the base. The plant is rather small and low-growing in the roadside grass. The leaves are more finely divided than the creeping buttercup, and sharply pointed. The sepals are pale, not reflexed, and fall off quickly. The stems are smooth, not hairy, and the stalks furrowed or ridged.

June – July.

1.

2.

3.

4.

PLATE 84

1 Greater Spearwort *Ranunculus lingua* **Ranunculaceae**
This resembles the Lesser Spearwort, but is a much larger plant with brighter yellow flowers.
The basal leaves, oval or cordate, are produced in autumn and are often submerged,
disappearing before the plant is in flower. The stem leaves are lance-shaped.

Common in wet places, marshes and fens. June — September.

2 Celery-leaved Crowfoot *Ranunculus sceleratus* **Ranunculaceae**
Annual or over-wintering. The stout stem is erect, hollow and furrowed. The shiny lower
leaves are long-stalked and palmately three-lobed, the stem leaves short-stemmed or sessile
with fewer and narrower segments. The flowers are small, the petals scarcely exceeding the
reflexed sepals, and are in a much-branched inflorescence. The achenes are in a conspicuously
long head.

Common in the south in damp muddy places at the edges of ponds. June — September.

3 Hairy Buttercup *Ranunculus sardous* **Ranunculaceae**
Annual. This resembles the Bulbous Buttercup but does not have stem tubers. The numerous pale
yellow flowers have reflexed sepals and furrowed stalks. The basal leaves are shiny, stalked, deeply
three-lobed and further cut, the terminal leaflet having a longer stalk. Leaves and stems are all hairy.
The achenes are brownish and have a ring of warts or tubercles inside the thick green border.

Rather local, southern and mainly coastal, in damp places. June — October.

1.

2.

3.

PLATE 85

1   Bulbous Buttercup   *Ranunculus bulbosus*   Ranunculaceae

The erect hairy stem rises from a corm-like basal tuber; there are no runners. The plant is perennial and dies down in midsummer and remains dormant until autumn. It is distinguished by its pale yellowish sepals being strongly reflexed.

Dry pastures and grassy slopes, often by the sea. Abundant in the south but less common in the north. May — June.

2   Meadow Buttercup   *Ranunculus acris*   Ranunculaceae

The tallest of the buttercups, this has a much-branched hairy stem and is not stoloniferous. The flowers are rather cup-shaped, sepals erect. The narrow stem leaves are three-lobed and deeply cut, having a ferny appearance; the basal leaves are less divided.

Meadows and pastures. June — July.

3   Creeping Buttercup *Ranunculus repens*   Ranunculaceae

The commonest buttercup, with long tenacious roots and many leafy runners which spread and root at the nodes, forming a thick carpet in damp meadows, pastures and woods, and also as a pernicious garden weed. The flowers are deep yellow, and the leaves stalked, three-lobed with wide toothed lobes; the mid lobe is stalked. Hairy.

May — August.

P<small>LATE</small> 86

1 Spiny-fruited Buttercup *Ranunculus muricatus* **Ranunculaceae**
Annual. A leafy plant about two feet high, with erect stems ending in a cluster of small yellow flowers. The flower-stalks lengthen as the fruits develop; these are the usual tight clusters of achenes, which end in a long curved spine. The stem leaves are large, 3-lobed, sharply toothed, with leafy bracts clasping the base. The basal leaves are long-stalked and very large, ending in a large, rounded lobe with smaller, unstalked, rounded leaflets along the stalk, decreasing in size and becoming very small at the base. It is uncommon, and rather local, but can spread quickly.

Roadsides, grassy shaded banks. May – July.

PLATE 87

1   Globe Flower, Lucken Gowan   *Trollius europaeus*   Ranunculaceae
Perennial. The large yellow sepals curve round into a ball, concealing the nectaries, the carpels, and the large boss of stamens. The flowers are usually solitary, but occasionally the stem branches, with one or two smaller flowers. The palmate leaves are deeply cut, with from three to five notched lobes; they clasp the stem but the basal leaves are stalked. Damp grassy places, mountain meadows, especially in the west where they grow abundantly and in great brilliance.

May — July.

2   Lesser Celandine   *Ranunculus ficaria*   Ranunculaceae
The flowers are brilliantly glossy, their eight to twelve petals open wide to the sun, but remain closed in dull weather. The stems are smooth and branching, occasionally with bulbils at the base of the leaf-stalks, and the leaves are smooth, heart-shaped and rather fleshy. At the base of the plant there is a cluster of root-tubers by which it spreads rapidly, forming a golden carpet which is one of the sights of a sunny day in early spring. It is perennial.

March — May.

3   Coltsfoot   *Tussilago farfara*   Compositae
Among the very first of the spring flowers comes the perennial coltsfoot with its daisy-heads of numerous narrow ray florets, solitary on stems which are covered with long scales, and rise direct from the creeping rhizomes which spread into a dense mat. The leaves come up after the flower, directly from the rhizomes, and are large, heart-shaped, with toothed edges, and purplish on the undersides.

Roadsides, banks and waste ground. March — April.

1.

2.

3.

PLATE 88

1   Goat's-beard   *Tragopogon pratensis* ssp. *minor*   Compositae

The stems are tall, erect, little-branched and slightly woolly when young. The lower leaves are very long and smooth, narrowing to a point almost like a grass; they clasp the stems and have conspicuous white veins. The solitary, bright yellow flower-heads are long-stalked, with a swelling beneath the head, and have eight or more lance-shaped, red-edged bracts, about twice as long as the florets. The flowers open only in the morning, hence its name of 'jack-go-to-bed-at-noon'. The seed-heads are large and handsome and the seeds have long beaks ending in a conspicuous feathery pappus.

Roadsides, waste land, grassy places, dunes. May — July.

2   Dandelion   *Taraxacum officinale*   Compositae

This very well-known plant with its bright golden flowers is so common everywhere that it comes as a surprise to learn that there are over a hundred different 'microspecies', all, it must be said, very similar. The large flower-head which is composed of many strap-shaped ray florets, is solitary on a smooth hollow stalk which bleeds a white milky juice when broken. Below the flower-head are two rows of bracts, the inner ones being long, linear and enclosing the ripening seeds, the outer or lower ones sharply reflexed. When ripe the seeding head appears as the familiar 'dandelion clock', the white umbrella-like pappus on each achene forming part of the silvery ball soon dispersed by the wind. The leaves form a flat rosette; they are long, sharply lobed, with a prominent mid-rib, and are very variable, broad or narrow. The tap-root is very long and deep-rooting.

Fields, roadsides, waste ground and gardens. March — October.

1.

2.

PLATE 89

1   Tansy   *Tanacetum vulgare*   **Compositae**

The button-shaped flowers are in large, rather flat clusters at the ends of the tough, stiffly erect stems. The leaves are pinnate, sharply toothed, and fern-like, with a strong aromatic scent and a bitter taste. They grow alternately along the stem, half-clasping it, giving the plant a bushy appearance.

Grassy places, often by deserted cottages, as this was an old garden herb. July — October.

2   Groundsel   *Senecio vulgaris*   **Compositae**

One of the commonest garden weeds. The flowers are small, normally without any ray florets, and almost hidden by the tubular involucre of bracts, the outer black-tipped at the ends. In fruit they become fluffy balls of airborne seeds. The leaves, which half-clasp the stems, are pinnate with narrow toothed lobes and have a ragged appearance. The erect stems are succulent but weak, and are often supported by other vegetation.

In flower all the year.

3   Ragwort   *Senecio jacobaea*   **Compositae**

The flowers have widely spaced, rather narrow ray florets of bright yellow with the disc florets deeper in colour and turning brown as they fade. The outer bracts are much shorter than the long dark-tipped inner ones. The flowers are in close branched clusters at the ends of tall stems which are branched from half-way up. The leaves are dark green, pinnately lobed and deeply cut with the end of the lobe blunt. The stem leaves are unstalked and have small wings where they clasp the stems.

   The plant has a ragged look, but it grows in such masses that it spreads a sheet of gold over old pastures, waste land, waysides and sand-dunes.

   The more uncommon Rayless Ragwort, *Senecio jacobaea* var. *nudus* is illustrated and described on the following page.

July — September.

4   Oxford Ragwort   *Senecio squalidus*   **Compositae**

Usually annual. This is spreading and branching, more lax in habit than the common Ragwort. The flower-head, too, is more loose and irregular, and the bright yellow ray florets are broader. The inner involucre bracts are long, but the outer are very short; all are conspicuously black-tipped. The lower leaves narrow into a winged stalk, the upper being half-clasping. They are smooth but very variable, some only toothed, others deeply lobed, but both sharply pointed. An introduced plant, but spreading rapidly.

Old walls, railway banks, waste ground, in the south. June — December.

1.

2.-

3.

4.

PLATE 90

1   Ragwort, Rayless Form   *Senecio jacobaea* **var.** *nudus*   **Compositae**
This can reach the same height as the common Ragwort, but the flowers are without ray florets, or occasionally with only one or two. The leaves are similarly deeply lobed and toothed and clasp the stem, the segments pointing upwards. The inner involucral bracts are black-tipped.

Grassy banks and waste ground. Not common.

2   Marsh Ragwort   *Senecio aquaticus*   **Compositae**
Biennial. The erect, often purplish, stems end in a spreading, loosely-branched inflorescence of golden-yellow flower-heads that are larger than those of the common Ragwort. The leaves are pinnately lobed, the upper being narrow and clasping, the basal leaves much larger, long-stalked, with a very large end lobe.

Marshes, wet meadows and ditches. July — August.

1.

2.

PLATE 91

1   Corn Marigold, Gule   *Chrysanthemum segetum*   Compositae
Annual. Erect stems, branching, and with rather widely spaced clasping stem leaves which are narrow, pointed and glaucous. The lower leaves are narrowed into a winged stalk, and may be coarsely toothed. The flower-heads are solitary with broad ray-florets, the bracts are ovate, glaucous, with broad, pale brown, dry margins, the stalk thickens below the flower-head. Although probably an introduced plant it is widespread and was a common weed of cultivated land, at one time turning cornfields golden long before harvest. An old rhyme runs:

> *'The Gule, the Gordon and the Hoodie Craw,*
> *Are the three warst things that Moray ever saw.'*

Now it is less common, more often confined to railway embankments and roadsides. June – August.

2   Golden-rod   *Solidago virgaurea* Compositae
An erect perennial, rather woody, leafy and often branching, with short flowering branches rising from the axils of the leaves, mostly clustered at the head of the stem. The leaves are long and lance-shaped. The yellow flower-heads are shortly stalked, with sparse ray-florets. Plants are variable, with distinctive dwarf forms found on mountains.

Common in dry grassy places, rocks and cliffs. July – September

1.

2.

PLATE 92

1   Carline Thistle   *Carlina vulgaris*   **Compositae**
Biennial. The long tap-root produces in the first year a rosette of stalkless, spiny, lance-shaped leaves, with wavy margins, cottony below. These die back before the plant flowers in the second season. The stiff erect flowering stems have shorter, half-clasping leaves which also have waved and spiny margins. The flower-heads are solitary and have an outer ring of spiny, leaf-like bracts, and an inner one of long, narrow, straw-coloured bracts resembling ray-florets. In the centre are the small brownish-yellow tube-florets. The fruits are achenes with rusty hairs and a long feathered pappus. The withered flower-heads with their yellow centres are often conspicuous throughout winter.

Calcareous grassland mainly in the south. July – October.

2   Common Fleabane   *Pulicaria dysenterica*   **Compositae**
A perennial of medium height, erect, hairy and branched, with stolons. The stem leaves are downy, narrowly oblong and wavy-edged, cordate-based, and clasp the stem. The flower-head is golden-yellow, with numerous narrow ray-florets which appear like a fringe around the large circle of disk-florets. The bracts at the base of the flower-head are narrow, scarious-tipped, hairy and sticky.

Marshes, wet meadows, ditches. South Scotland. August – September.

3   Marsh Cudweed   *Gnaphalium uliginosum* syn. *Filaginella uliginosa*   **Compositae**
A very woolly annual much branched from the base. The leaves are narrowly oblong and woolly on both sides. The flower-heads of brownish-yellow florets, overtopped by the leaves at their base, have woolly bracts which are pale below with dark chaffy tips. They are in dense terminal clusters of three to ten. There are several other Cudweeds, all more or less woolly, with similar flowers.

Damp grasslands and paths, acid soils, common. July – September.

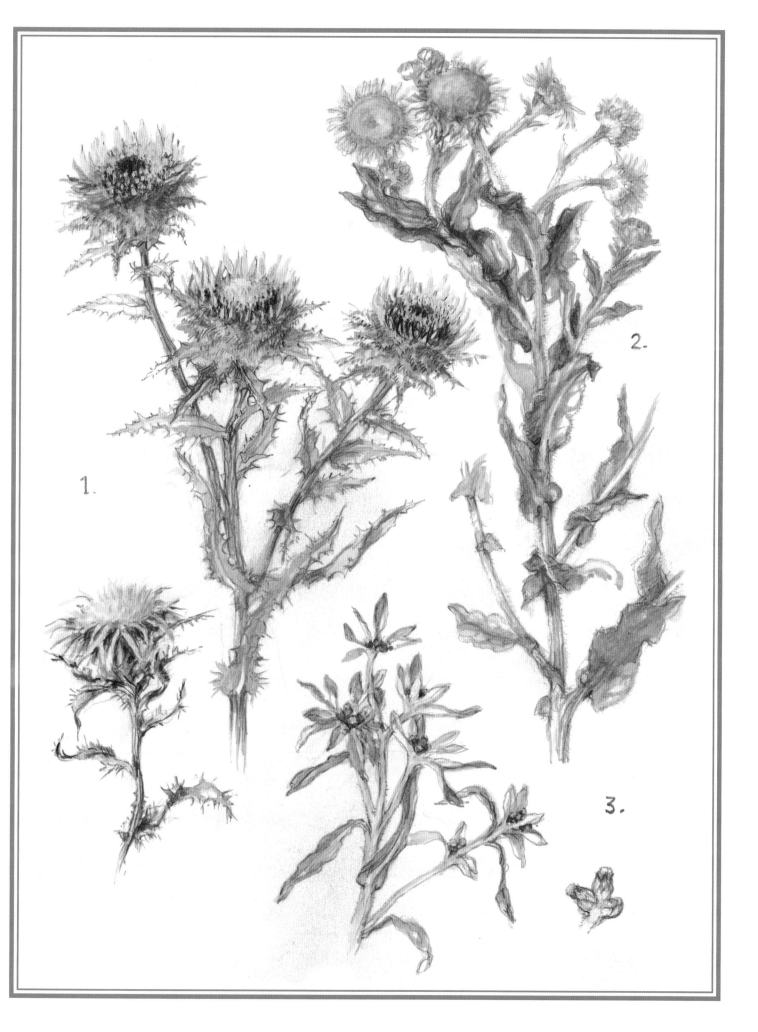

1.

2.

3.

PLATE 93

1   Nodding Bur-marigold   *Bidens cernua*   **Compositae**
An annual with simple or slightly branching stems and long, narrow, coarsely-toothed, unstalked, pale green leaves. The drooping, long-stalked, yellow flower-heads are solitary, with no ray-florets, but with a whorl of leaf-like outer bracts; the inner bracts are much smaller, ovate and dark-streaked. A plant of ponds and stream-sides, and especially of places with standing water in winter but not in summer.

Mostly in southern Scotland, but rare. July – October.

2   Tripartite Bur-marigold   *Bidens tripartita*   **Compositae**
An annual with erect branching stems. The leaves, which narrow into a short winged stalk, are opposite, trifoliate with lance-shaped toothed lobes, the terminal leaflet broader and often three-lobed. The solitary, long-stalked flower-heads are more or less erect, and, as above, have leaf-like outer bracts and ovate brownish inner bracts, with yellow disk-florets.

Reaching north as far as Moray and Kintyre. Rare. July – September.

1.

2.

PLATE 94

1   Nipplewort   *Lapsana communis*   Compositae
Erect, slender, branching and leafy stems bear branched clusters of pale yellow flowers with only eight to ten florets. The upper leaves are lanceolate and short-stalked, the lower ones lyre-shaped with a very large terminal lobe and small lateral lobes. All are thin and may be smooth or hairy.

A common annual of waysides, hedges, wood-margins and waste places. July — September.

2   Common Hawkweed   *Hieracium vulgatum*   Compositae
Hawkweeds form a very large genus with a bewildering number of species, all perennial, which have been divided into a large number of sections. The specimen shown is one of the commonest species. There are few rosette leaves, the stem leaves are lance-shaped, the lowest stalked; all are toothed with forward-pointing teeth. The flower-heads are solitary on short stalks in a loose inflorescence, yellow, with hairy lance-shaped bracts.

Woods, banks, walls and rocks. July — August.

3   Orange Hawkweed   *Hieracium aurantiacum* syn. *Pilosella aurantiaca*   Compositae
Also known as 'Fox and Cubs' and 'Grim the Collier'. This has a few stem leaves as well as the basal rosette, and is tall and hairy (stalks, stems and bracts especially with black hairs). There is a branching inflorescence of brick-red flower-heads in close clusters. This is a garden escape (C. Europe) which has become extensively naturalised. It is noticeable with its bright colouring and is therefore included here.

Roadsides and waste ground. July — August.

1.

2.

3.

PLATE 95

1   Prickly Sow-thistle   *Sonchus asper*   **Compositae**
An erect, usually branched, hairless and widespread annual with an open cluster of bright yellow flower-heads at the top of a tall ribbed stem. These, like so many others with dandelion-like flowers, have only ray-florets; they are all rather similar and very confusing. Here the leaves are distinctive. The upper leaves are long and tapering, slightly lobed, with sharp, spiny margins, and clasp the stem with rounded, spiny, basal lobes. The lower leaves are stalked.

Cultivated ground, waysides and waste ground. May – September.

2   Smooth Hawksbeard   *Crepis capillaris*   **Compositae**
A slender, nearly hairless, much branched annual or biennial. The rather small flower-heads are in a spreading, open cluster; they have two rows of bracts, the upper long and pointed, the lower only one third as long. The narrow upper leaves clasp the stem with arrow-shaped lobes, and point upwards, giving the plant a narrow appearance. The lower leaves are much larger, also long and narrow but with deeply cut, tapering, pointed lobes.

Waste ground, grasslands, waysides. June – September.

3 Mouse-ear Hawkweed   *Pilosella officinarum*   **syn.** *Hieracium pilosella*   **Compositae**
A rosette-forming perennial with creeping stolons which have small narrow leaves at intervals. The rosette leaves are blunt and untoothed, dark green above and white-felted below. The solitary flower heads are pale yellow, the outer florets reddish-tipped outside, with sharply pointed involucre.

Common in grasslands, banks, heaths. May – August.

PLATE 96

1   Perennial Sow-thistle   *Sonchus arvensis*   Compositae
The widespread creeping roots bear erect stems, very tall and robust, 60–150cm, hollow and furrowed, cottony below and glandular-hairy above. The large basal leaves have rather triangular, spiny lobes with a pointed tip, and narrowing into a winged stalk. The uppermost stem leaves are narrow, scarcely lobed, while the lower, much larger, long, lobed and spiny, clasp the stem; all are shiny green. The flower-heads are in a loose leafless cluster (corymb), and bracts and flower stalks are covered with yellow glandular hairs. The involucre is bell-shaped.

Waste land, hedge-banks, arable ground, very common. July – October.

2   Catsear   *Hypochaeris radicata*   Compositae
The solitary flower-heads rise on leafless stems from a rosette of toothed or lobed leaves, rather like dandelion leaves. The flower-heads have a hollow swollen stem immediately below the head, and the involucral bracts are long, lance-shaped and pointed.

Dry pastures, open woodlands. June – September.

1.

2.

PLATE 97

1   Tuberous Comfrey   *Symphytum tuberosum*   Boraginaceae

A sturdy, leafy and hairy perennial plant, with a tuberous stout rhizome, and bristly, unwinged stems, sometimes with short branches near the top. The upper leaves are unstalked, the middle leaves the largest with short stalks, and the lower ones small and narrowed at the base; all are hairy and deeply veined. The creamy yellow flowers are narrowly tubular, in one-sided clusters with the buds in a tight coil. The calyx has five sharply pointed lobes, about one third the length of the tube. Also cultivated in early times as a healing herb for sprains, bruises and cuts, and to assist in uniting broken bones. Old names include 'Knitbone', 'Bruisewort' and 'Bone-set'.

Damp woods and hedge banks, commonest in the north. June – July.

2   Henbane   *Hyoscyamus niger*   Solanaceae

Annual or biennial, a tall plant with a stout, sticky-hairy, strong-smelling stem and leaves. The stem leaves are unstalked and entire with wavy margins and pointed teeth, the lower leaves being stalked. The flowers have five unequal lobes joining into a tube to which the five purple anthers are attached. They are yellow, densely netted with purple veins, and are closely set along the stem in two axillary rows. The five-pointed calyx enlarges to enclose the rounded fruit. It is a very poisonous plant.

Sandy places, especially by the sea, and on disturbed ground in farmyards, waste ground. May – September.

1.

2.

PLATE 98

1 Wallflower *Erysimum cheiri* **syn.** *Cheiranthus cheiri* **Cruciferae**
The erect woody stem is crowded with narrow, almost sessile, lanceolate leaves, and ends in a close raceme of bright yellow fragrant flowers, which lengthens as the long, narrow, flattened fruits develop. Short, flowering side branches grow along the stem.

This is an introduced perennial plant, which is now well established on walls and ruins. Less common in the north. May – June.

2 Hedge Mustard *Sisymbrium officinale* **Cruciferae**
The stiff, erect stem branches at the top into several erect subsidiary stems with small flowers and short-stemmed narrow fruits held close to the stem and pointing upwards. The basal leaves are in a rosette and are deeply pinnately-lobed with a longer terminal lobe, while in the stem leaves the terminal lobe is long and narrow.

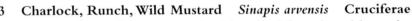

A common annual weed of arable land, waste places, roadsides. June – July.

3 Charlock, Runch, Wild Mustard *Sinapis arvensis* **Cruciferae**
An erect, medium tall, hairy annual, with stalked, lyre-shaped lower leaves and sessile, lanceolate upper leaves. The flowers are bright yellow with spreading sepals.

   This used to be a common weed of arable land, turning fields golden, especially spring-sown crops on calcareous and heavy soils, but less now with weed control.

May – July.

4 Flixweed *Descurainia sophia* **Cruciferae**
Annual or overwintering, with erect stems, and much divided, pinnate, lacy, grey-green leaves. The narrow flowers have pale yellow petals almost as long as the sepals. The narrow fruits are on very slender, upward-pointing stalks.

Roadsides and waste places except for much of the north and west, but nowhere very common. June – August.

PLATE 99

1   Yellow Horned Poppy   *Glaucium flavum*   **Papaveraceae**
Perennial. From a long stout tap-root there rises a large rosette of intensely glaucous leaves which are rough and hairy, stalked, long and pinnately lobed, the lobes pointing various ways and coarsely toothed. The upper leaves half-clasp the stems which are erect, branching, and also glaucous. The short-stalked flowers are large and yellow, with four petals. The pod is very long, up to 30cm, narrow, rough and curving, giving the plant its name.

Sand and shingle, on the extreme southern coasts of Scotland, around Berwick and reaching to Kincardine. June — September.

2   Greater Celandine *Chelidonium majus*   **Papaveraceae**
An annual, of medium height, with branching brittle stems which exude bright orange-yellow juice when broken. The leaves are almost pinnate with oval leaflets, the end one often three-lobed; all are crenate-toothed and glaucous underneath. The small four-petalled flowers are bright yellow with four pale greenish-yellow sepals which quickly fall off as the buds open. The capsule lengthens and is narrow and constricted, containing black seeds.

Banks, hedges, walls, often near houses. May — September.

1.

2.

PLATE 100

1   Pepper Saxifrage   *Silaum silau*s   Umbelliferae
An erect and branching perennial with a stout woody tap-root and slender ridged stems. The lower leaves are two or three times pinnate with narrow pointed segments giving an open lacy effect. The segments are extremely finely toothed. The upper leaves are few and small. The small yellow flowers are in long-stalked crowded umbels. The fruits are egg-shaped, shiny and brownish-purple when ripe.

Local in meadows and grassy banks as far north as Fife. June — August.

2   Rock Samphire   *Crithmum maritimum*   Umbelliferae
An almost woody perennial with solid ridged stems sheathed by short stalked fleshy leaves with narrow succulent lobes. The creamy flowers are in umbels with many bracts and bracteoles, and the fruits are corky, oval and ridged, sometimes purplish. The plant forms large clumps with showy frothing masses of pale flowers against the rocks and cliffs of the coasts.

Mostly in the south but as far north as Ayr. June — August.

3   Saltwort   *Salsola kali*   Chenopodiaceae
A prostrate and branching prickly annual with pale green or reddish-striped stems. The stalkless linear succulent leaves narrow into a little sharp spine at the tip. The tiny greenish-yellow flowers are usually solitary in the axil of a leaf, each with two leaf-like bracteoles and three stamens and five sepals.

On sandy shores along the drift line. July — September.

PLATE 101

1   Mountain Pansy   *Viola lutea*   Violaceae
The large solitary flowers, on long slender stalks, are usually yellow, but are variable and have
a wide colour range, even deep purple forms being found. The stems rise from a creeping
rhizome with leaves and stipules surrounding the flower stalks. Perennial.

Grassy places on hills and mountains. June − August.

2   Seaside Pansy   *Viola tricolor* ssp. *curtisii*   Violaceae
A small plant with slender, rather prostrate, branched stems, which often
grow under the sand, producing little tufts of leaves at intervals. The
flowers have wide petals, long spurs and a very small calyx. Leaves and
stipules are similar to those of the tri-colour Pansy (*Viola tricolor*).

*Rather rare, sand-dunes on west and south-west coasts and on the Hebrides.
May − July.*

3   Field Pansy   *Viola arvensis*   Violaceae
A variable small annual with tiny flowers, cream or pale yellow with deep orange centres, and
petals shorter than the sepals. The stem leaves are oval and toothed, with narrow, leafy stipules.
The plant has a bushy appearance.

Cultivated fields and waste ground. April − November.

1.

1.

2.

3.

PLATE 102

1   Marsh Violet   *Viola palustris*   Violaceae
Perennial. The flowers are small, rounded, and very pale lilac with darker veinings, and have short, blunt spurs and tiny bracts midway on flower stalks. The kidney-shaped leaves rise from a long, creeping rhizome.

Bogs, marshes, wet heaths. April – July.

2   Heartsease, Wild Pansy   *Viola tricolor*   Violaceae
The flowers of this little pansy are very variable in colour, usually in shades of violet and blue, pale and dark, with the two upper petals always darkest, occasionally one finds variations with white and with yellow colours. The lower leaves are oval and lobed, the upper are narrow, lobed, and have pointed stipules.

It is a common annual, or perennial, on both cultivated and waste ground, on short grassland and in hilly districts. April – October.

3   Common Violet   *Viola riviniana*   Violaceae
The flowers are blue-violet, with broad petals, and a pale almost white spur rounded at the tip; they have no scent. The leaves are heart-shaped and there are toothed stipules where their stalks join the branching stem.

It is perennial and common in woods, hedgebanks, and on mountains. March – May.

1.

2.

3.

PLATE 103

1 Hairy Violet *Viola hirta* **Violaceae**

This has fine spreading hairs on the leaves, stalks and capsules. There are no leafy stems or runners but all leaves and flower stems rise directly from the rootstock. The flowers are lilac-blue with a large white centre, and are unscented; the sepals are short and blunt. The leaves are narrow, rather triangular and cordate at the base, and enlarge greatly in size as they age.

Calcareous grassy places, dunes, in the south. March – May.

2 Sweet Violet *Viola odorata* **Violaceae**

This perennial violet has long rooting runners and large, broad, glossy leaves which become larger in summer. Leaves and flowers rise from the rootstock. The flowers are dark violet, sometimes white, and are fragrant. The sepals and violet spur are rather blunt, and the whole plant is downy. It is rare in the north, more frequent in the south but only local.

Woods and hedgerows. March – May.

3 Heath Dog Violet *Viola canina* **Violaceae**

Distinguished by its colour, which is pure clear blue without any lilac. The spur is straight, blunt and yellowish, and the sepals are long, narrow and pointed. The leaves are oval lance-shaped with rounded bases. It has long creeping stems and no basal rosette.

Heaths, dry grassland, dunes, but rather local. April – June.

1.

2.

3.

PLATE 104

1 Heath Speedwell *Veronica officinalis* **Scrophulariaceae**
The flowers are small, pale lilac and veined, in spikes rising erect from the leaf axils, and carried well above the leaves. The leaves are in pairs, oval or rounded, downy and slightly toothed. The stems creep and root at the nodes, and are hairy all round.

Dry heaths and open woods. May – August.

2 Germander Speedwell *Veronica chamaedrys* **Scrophulariaceae**
The sprays of bright blue flowers are on long stems rising from the axils of the upper leaves; each is stalked, with a corolla of four unequal lobes, the upper largest, and a white centre. The leaves are oval, stalkless, hairy and coarsely toothed, and grow in pairs at intervals along the stem, which is at first prostrate and rooting at the nodes, then rising erect with the flowering stems, which have white hairs in two lines on opposite sides, being smooth between.

Very common, woods, hedges, banks, roadsides. March – August.

3 Common Field Speedwell, *Veronica persica* **Scrophulariaceae**
   Buxbaum's Speedwell
Although an introduced species this has become one of the commonest weeds of cultivated land. The flowers are almost the size of those of the Germander Speedwell, but are bright sky-blue with a prominent white centre and lower lobe. They are solitary on slender stalks from the axils of the leaves. The fruit is a distinctive capsule with two divergent lobes.

All spring and summer.

1.

2.

3.

PLATE 105

1 Ivy-leaved Speedwell *Veronica hederifolia* **Scrophulariaceae**
An annual, spreading, low and hairy, with light green leaves, ivy-shaped with rounded lobes, set alternately along the stem and stalks. The solitary, pale lilac flowers are in the leaf axils, tiny and short-stalked, but the stalk lengthens as the fruit ripens.

A weed of gardens and arable land. April – July.

2 Wall Speedwell *Veronica arvensis* **Scrophulariaceae**
An annual, erect, downy and very variable in size, sometimes branched at the base with ascending branches. The tiny, bright blue flowers are in terminal racemes, with lance-shaped bracts longer than the flower, the lower of these gradually pass into the stem leaves, which are oval, coarsely toothed and in opposite pairs. The flower stalks are very short. The fruit, like most speedwells, is a flattened, two-lobed capsule.

Common in dry grassland, heaths, and in cultivated ground. March – October.

3 Thyme-leaved Speedwell *Veronica serpyllifolia* **Scrophulariaceae**
This is perennial, with stems creeping and rooting at the nodes, but becoming erect to flower in terminal racemes. The flowers are pale blue or whitish, with darker lines on the upper lobe. The leaves, oval, rounded at the ends, are very shortly stalked or stalkless.

Grassland, heaths, waste places, often a garden weed. March – October.

4 Brooklime *Veronica beccabunga* **Scrophulariaceae**
Smooth and fleshy, with thick stems that creep and root. The racemes of small, bright blue flowers rise from the axils of the leaves which are in opposite pairs and are rounded, thick, fleshy and shiny, with short stalks.

A common plant of streams and shallow water. Perennial. July – August.

1.

2.

3.

4.

PLATE 106

1   Ivy-leaved Toadflax   *Cymbalaria muralis*   Scrophulariaceae
A low-growing plant with slender purplish trailing and rooting stems. The leaves are ivy-shaped, thick and smooth, with long thin stalks. In the leaf axils the small lilac flowers are solitary on slender stalks. They are two-lipped, the upper lip two-lobed with dark lines, the lower wider and three-lobed, and between is the rounded white 'palate' with yellow spot at the mouth. Although not a native plant it has become naturalised and common on old walls and ruins.

In flower most of the year.

2   Field Gentian   *Gentianella campestris*   Gentianaceae
An erect leafy little plant with the flowers rising from the axils of the leaves and pointing upward along the stem. The leaves are broadly lance-shaped. The lilac-blue flowers have four lobes and a fringe of white hairs in the centre. The calyx is divided into four lobes, the two outer large and overlapping, almost hiding the two small inner ones.

Pastures and dunes, common. July – September.

3   Felwort, Autumn Gentian   *Gentianella amarella*   Gentianaceae
A biennial which produces in the first year a rosette of oblong leaves which then die in autumn. The subsequent flowering stems are simple or branching with broadly lance-shaped leaves, resembling *Gentianella campestri*s, but the flower has five dull purple lobes and the calyx lobes are almost equal and much shorter than the corolla tube. There are a number of recognisable sub-species.

Dry pastures and dunes, usually calcareous. August – October.

4   Skull-cap   *Scutellaria galericulata*   Labiatae
The erect smooth stems, square in section, rise from a creeping rhizome. The paired leaves are oval, pointed, cordate at the base and shallowly lobed. A pair of blue-violet flowers rises from the leaf axils. Each has a two-lipped reddish calyx and a long corolla tube, slightly curved below.

Edges of burns, fens, wet woods. June – September.

5   Lesser Skull-cap   *Scutellaria minor*   Labiatae
Very similar to *S. galericulata* but smaller. The leaves are tinged with purple beneath. The flowers, also in pairs, are more of a pinkish-purple with a straight tube, and have many dark spots on the lip.

Wet heaths up to 1500 feet, local and rather rare. Absent north-east of Stirling. July – October.

3.

1.

2.

5.

4.

PLATE 107

1   Mint   *Mentha* **spp.   Labiatae**

Mints inter-breed readily and are therefore difficult to distinguish. The illustration shows a form close to *Mentha arvensis*, the Corn Mint. The small flowers with their projecting stamens are in close whorls widely spaced along the stem, with two leaf-like bracts below each cluster. The leaves are oval, stalked and toothed; the stems erect and reddish.

Fields and damp open places, very common. Perennial. May – September.

2   Wild Marjoram   *Origanum vulgare*   **Labiatae**

The small flowers are in rounded clusters at the ends of the branching stems, the deep pink buds open to pale lavender flowers with projecting stamens and purple bracts. The whole plant has a sweet aromatic scent. The stalked leaves are oval and downy, in pairs, entire or only very slightly toothed. The stems are erect and hairy.

Dry grassy places, especially on calcareous soils and on fixed dunes. July – September.

3   Water Mint   *Mentha aquatica*   **Labiatae**

Variable, but the upper two or three whorls of flowers form a rounded terminal head. The stems are erect and often purplish; the stalked leaves are usually a pointed oval.

Marshes, near streams and ponds. Perennial. July – October.

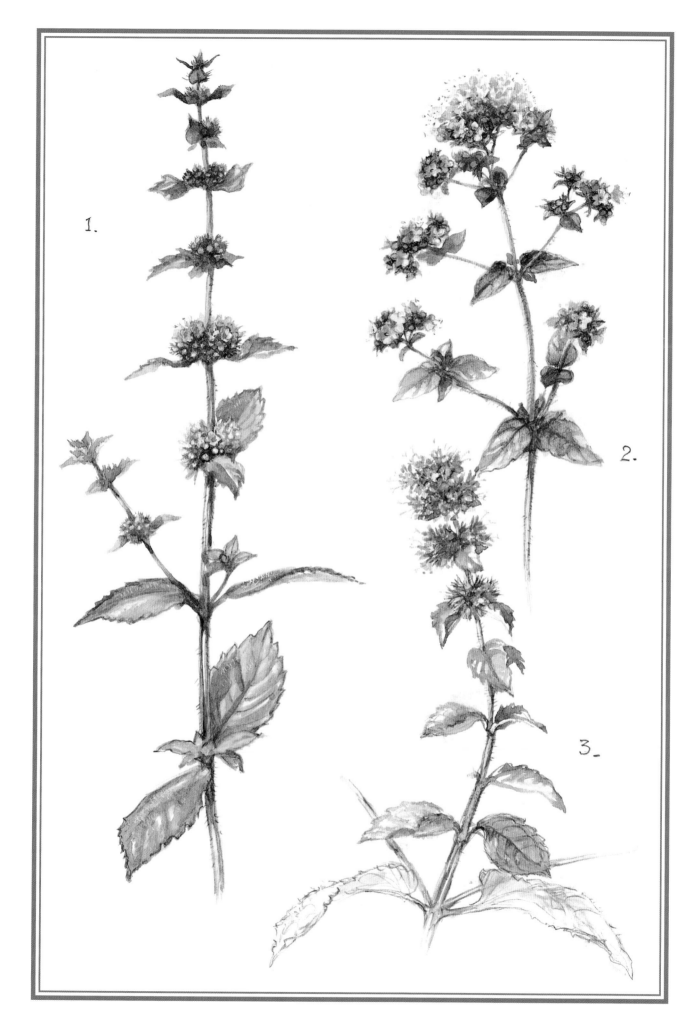

1.

2.

3.

PLATE 108

1   Pyramidal Bugle   *Ajuga pyramidalis*   Labiatae

This differs from *Ajuga reptans* in having the stem hairy all round, in having pale mauve flowers that are longer and rather narrower, with protruding stamens, and in the upper stem leaves being much longer than the flowers. Also the plant has stolons, but no runners. The leaves are similar in shape and colouring, or even more purplish and darker.

Crevices of base-rich rocks in the west. May – July.

2   Bugle   *Ajuga reptans*   Labiatae

The small, bright blue flowers are tubular and two-lipped, the upper lip very short and the lower wide, with rounded lobes marked with white; they are in close whorls in the axils of the stem leaves. The stem is short, square, and hairy on two sides. The leaves are oval with slightly rounded teeth, and often bronzy, stalkless on the stem and in alternate pairs. At the base of the plant the leaves are stalked and form a rosette, with runners radiating out which lie on the ground and root at the tips. The whole plant tends to have a purplish or bronzy look especially as it grows older.

Common in damp woods and grassy places. May – July.

1.

2.

PLATE 109

1 Self-heal *Prunella vulgaris* Labiatae

The violet flowers are two-lipped, the upper lip forming a pronounced hood. They are in a short dense spike on an erect branch, with smaller secondary branches, rising from a low creeping stem. The calyx is also two-lipped with two distinct teeth on the lower lip. Each whorl of flowers has broad, pointed, pale green bracts below, edged with purple. The leaves are in pairs, ovate and hairy, often with reddish margins. The stem is square, ridged and reddish, creeping and rooting from a short rhizome.

Perennial. Grassy places, clearings in woods, waste ground. June – November.

2 Ground Ivy *Glechoma hederacea* Labiatae

The small tubular flowers, violet with crimson markings on the lower lip, are in axillary whorls. The leaves are kidney-shaped, long-stalked, with regular rounded teeth, and are often purplish, especially at the top of the flower stalk. It is a low, creeping plant with long, square and reddish rooting stems which soon carpet the ground, and bear erect flowering stalks. The plant is strongly aromatic.

Woods and waste ground, usually on damp and heavy soil. March – June.

3 Common Milkwort *Polygala vulgaris* Polygalaceae

A small perennial plant, slender and woody at the base and branching with erect stems at the end of which are rather long spikes of small flowers dangling on short stalks. The flowers are usually blue, sometimes pale lilac, pink or white. The flower has five sepals, the two inner being large and coloured like the petals, and covering the three true petals which are joined at the base and attached to the stamens. The three outer sepals are tiny and green. The leaves are small, lance-shaped, and are borne alternately up the stem.

Grassy places and heaths. May – September.

4 Heath Milkwort *Polygala serpyllifolia* Polygalaceae

This is like *Polygala vulgaris* but is smaller and more slender. The flowers are deep purple-blue or dark pink and are in short spikes. The leaves are more rounded, closely set and often opposite at the foot of the stem.

There are many varieties and subspecies of Milkwort, basically similar, but differing in size or detail of flowers and leaves.

Common on heaths and peaty moors, not on lime. May – September.

5 Field Madder *Sherardia arvensis* Rubiaceae

A small, scrambling, weak-stemmed annual, with whorls of short lance-shaped leaves, usually five, at intervals along the stems. The flowers are in terminal heads of four to eight, pale lilac, with four petals and a long tube. The sepals are very short. Below the flower-head there is a ruff of leaf-like bracts. Formerly a red dye extracted from the coloured roots was used to dye cloth.

Bare or cultivated ground. May – October.

PLATE 110

1 Bird's-eye Primrose *Primula farinosa* **Primulaceae**
A small perennial with several lilac flowers on short individual stalks, at the end of a slender stem, mealy when young. The flowers have a yellow eye, spreading lobes, and the calyx teeth are pointed. The leaves, in a basal rosette, are toothed, broadest near the tip, green above and very mealy beneath.

Damp grassy places on basic soil on hills and mountains in south Scotland. May – July.

2 Scottish Primrose *Primula scotica* **Primulaceae**
Endemic to Scotland, this is the smallest of the primroses. The tiny purple flowers, with short stalks and rounded calyx teeth, are grouped at the end of short stems rising from a rosette of small leaves. These are broadest in the middle and untoothed and mealy-white beneath. The whole plant is very mealy.

Short coastal turf and dunes, but only in the far north; Caithness, west Sutherland and Orkney. May – June and again July – August.

3 Wild Thyme *Thymus polytrichus* **syn.** *Thymus drucei* **Labiatae**
The flowering stems rise erect from the prostrate woody main stems which are creeping and mat-forming. The flowers are on tight rounded heads at the ends of the stems with varying shades of purple on different plants. The tiny oval leaves have very short stalks and are often woolly. The plant is very aromatic.

Heaths, dunes, dry sandy and grassy places, screes. June – September.

4 Common Eyebright *Euphrasia officinalis* **agg.** **Scrophulariaceae**
There are a great many species and hybrids of *Euphrasia* so that precise identification is very difficult. The stem in the plant illustrated is stiff, erect and branching with pairs of rounded, sharply toothed leaves or bracts at intervals. The flowers are in their axils, and are usually purplish. The upper lip has two rounded lobes which are notched, the lower lip is three-lobed with the central lobe longer, notched, and with a bright yellow spot near the throat. The fruit is flat and heart-shaped and contains many small yellow seeds.

Common on turf, heaths and on high ground. Annual. July – September.

1.

2.

3.

4.

PLATE 111

1   Meadow Cranesbill   *Geranium pratense*   **Geraniaceae**

A handsome perennial plant, tall, erect and branching, with pairs of blue-purple flowers, delicately veined with pink. The large leaves are palmate and deeply cut, those from the base long-stalked, those on the stems stalkless and having red stipules. The characteristic long-billed fruits hang down until completely ripe.

Roadsides and grassy places. June — September.

2   Wood Cranesbill   *Geranium sylvaticum*   **Geraniaceae**

Like the Meadow Cranesbill, but less robust, and the flowers are smaller, more reddish violet with white at base of the petals; they are more numerous but also in pairs. The stalks of individual flowers remain erect after flowering. The basal leaves are pale green and less deeply lobed.

Meadows, hedge-banks, damp woods and mountain rock ledges. June — July.

1.

2 -

PLATE 112

1 Wood Vetch *Vicia sylvatica* **Leguminosae**

Trailing perennial, with branching tendrils. The leaves have from six to nine pairs of oval leaflets with short, narrow points (mucronate) and stipules that are semi-circular with many narrow teeth at the base. The flowers, in one-sided racemes, are pale lilac or white, with purple veins.

Rocky, bushy places, woods, shingle and cliffs by the sea. June – August.

2 Purple Milk-vetch *Astragalus danicus* **Leguminosae**

Low-growing perennial, with a slender branched root-stock, and leaves and stems covered with soft white hairs. The leaves are pinnate, with many small oval leaflets and an end leaflet. The narrow, erect, purple flowers are in a close, clover-like cluster, with tiny bracts below them, at the end of a thin leafless stalk, longer than the leaves. The brown seed-pods are also erect, and covered with white hairs; each contains two seeds.

Short turf on calcareous soils and dunes in the east. May – July.

3 Tufted Vetch *Vicia cracca* **Leguminosae**

A climbing and scrambling perennial with branching tendrils. Many pairs of small lance-shaped leaflets are closely set along the leaf-stalk, the lowest being close to the stem beside the stipules. The drooping, bright purplish-blue flowers are in dense, long, one-sided racemes, and have minute, upper calyx teeth.

Grassy and bushy places, roadsides, where the massed flower-heads make vivid patches of colour. June – August.

1.

2.

3.

PLATE 113

1   Hairy Tare   *Vicia hirsuta*   Leguminosae
A slender trailing annual, with racemes of from one to eight tiny pale lilac flowers at the ends of long stalks. The leaves are pinnate with from four to eight pairs of narrow oblong leaflets, and end in branched tendrils. The small seed-pods are downy and usually contain two seeds.

Grassy places, cultivated land. June – August.

2   Spring Vetch   *Vicia lathyroides*   Leguminosae
A slender, downy and prostrate annual whose short leaves have only two to three pairs of narrow leaflets which widen to a blunt tip. There is no end leaflet, but occasionally a short unbranched tendril. At the base of the leaf there are small, half-arrow shaped stipules. The tiny flowers are solitary, rosy-lilac on opening but soon fading to lilac, and the pods are hairless.

Dry sandy ground, especially by the sea and mostly in the east. April – May.

3   Purple Oxytropis   *Oxytropis halleri*   Leguminosae
A softly hairy perennial with short branches rising direct from a stout rootstock, clothed with narrow persistent stipules. The leaves are pinnate and silky-hairy with about ten pairs of pointed oval leaflets. The flowers are in a short raceme on a leafless stem, pale purple, the keel tipped with dark purple, bright against their rocky background. The seed-pod is downy, with a pointed keel, containing numerous seeds.

Dry rocky pastures and mountain ledges up to 2,000ft. North Scotland, local and rare. June – July.

PLATE 114

1   Water Forget-me-not   *Myosotis scorpioides*   **Boraginaceae**
The sky-blue flowers, the largest of the family, are in loose clusters at the ends of the leafy stems, with the buds in a tight coil, and the stems elongating as the plant ages so that the stalked fruits are spaced out, each in its green five-pointed calyx. The leaves are oval, long and narrow, short-stalked at the base but stalkless on the stems which lie prostrate on the wet sides of streams and pools, or float on the water with the flower stems rising erect. The plants can form wide beds. Perennial.

June – September.

2   Wood Forget-me-not   *Myosotis sylvatica*   **Boraginaceae**
The flowers, smaller than those of the Water Forget-me-not, are in an inflorescence which elongates more markedly as flowers fade, and the calyx is distinctly hairy. The basal leaves are large and broad, but the upper are narrower, lanceolate; both are hairy on both surfaces.

Damp woods, more common in the south. May – June.

3   Lesser Water Forget-me-not,   *Myosotis laxa*   **Boraginaceae**
　　Tufted Forget-me-not   syn. *Myosotis caespitosa*
This has slender stems, erect in flower, and pale green stalkless leaves. The flowers are tiny, pale sky-blue, pinkish in bud, and the calyx has a flattened covering of hair.

Watery places. May – August.

4   Yellow-and-blue Forget-me-not   *Myosotis discolor*   **Boraginaceae**
Annual, with very tiny flowers, at first in a close coil, which open cream or pale yellow and change to blue; the stalks are very short. The leaves are narrow, unstalked on the stem, the lower ones narrowing at the base; all are hairy.

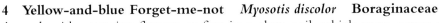

Common on light soils in grassy places. May – September.

5   Early Forget-me-not   *Myosotis ramosissima*   **Boraginaceae**
Annual. Very tiny, with minute, bright blue – never yellow – flowers. The tube is shorter than the calyx and the calyx teeth are spreading. The inflorescence is much longer than the leafy part of the stem.

Dry, sandy, open ground on coasts, sand-dunes, especially where vegetation is kept down by rabbits. April – May.

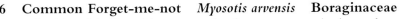

6   Common Forget-me-not   *Myosotis arvensis*   **Boraginaceae**
Annual – biennial. Branching stems rise from a rosette, the lower leaves stalked and rounded, the stem leaves long, narrow and unstalked, all hairy. The flowers are very small, bright blue, and the flowering stem becomes very long as it ages, spacing out the stalked seed-heads. Two stages of growth are common.

A common weed of gardens and cultivated ground, woods and sand-dunes. April – September.

PLATE 115

1   Alkanet   *Pentaglottis sempervirens*   Boraginaceae

The brilliant blue flowers have five rounded lobes and a conspicuous white centre, rather wheel-shaped and raised into a short tube. They are in small paired heads, each with a leafy bract below, on long stalks rising from the leaf-axils. The leaves are broad and pointed, rough and hairy, the lower ones stalked and very large. The stems are strong, erect and hollow, and are covered with stiff white hairs.

Widespread but local, and possibly native only in S W England. Woods. May — July.

2   Lesser Bugloss   *Anchusa arvensis* syn. *Lycopsis arvensis*   Boraginaceae

Also a rough bristly plant. The small flowers are sky-blue with white centres and the five lobes are joined into a long curved corolla tube, doubly bent. The leaves are lanceolate with undulating slightly toothed margins, and are covered with bristly hairs, the upper leaves clasping the stems, the lower stalked. The stems are rough and branching.

Edges of cultivated fields, waste land, damp roadside banks. June — September.

3   Oysterplant   *Mertensia maritima*   Boraginaceae

A perennial, prostrate, intensely glaucous plant, branching, hairless and fleshy. The oval leaves are covered with rough dots, the lower being stalked and the upper clasping the stem. The flowers are at the ends of the branches in a forking leafy inflorescence; they are bell-shaped, five-petalled, pink in bud and turning blue on opening.

Shingly sandy shores in the north and west, but apparently decreasing. June — August.

1

2.

3.

PLATE 116

1   Viper's Bugloss   *Echium vulgare*   Boraginaceae

Perennial, a very rough bristly plant with erect stems rising from a rosette of lance-shaped or oblong leaves which have a strong mid vein and are stalked. The stem leaves, also lance-shaped, are stalkless and rounded at the base. The flowers are in short, curving, almost stalkless clusters in the axils of the upper stem bracts or leaves, forming a long panicle. They are bright blue, funnel-shaped with unequal lobes and four long protruding stamens; the little round pink buds cluster below them. The calyx is short with narrow teeth which almost hide the fruit. Local, south Scotland.

Sandy places, cliffs, dunes. June — September.

2   Common Comfrey   *Symphytum officinale*   Boraginaceae

A robust, hairy, tall and leafy perennial with upright stems, which have a narrow wing running a short way down the stem from each leaf. The leaves are broadly lance-shaped, the lower stalked and very large. The drooping flowers are bell-shaped, usually mauve, and are at first in a tight coil. The hairy calyx has sharply pointed teeth. The fruits are shiny black nutlets. The Russian Comfrey, *Symphytum* x *uplandicum* has similar purple flowers but is a much taller plant, and is now very common.

Damp banks, marshy places. May — June.

1.

2.

PLATE 117

1   Devil's-bit Scabious   *Succisa pratensis*   Dipsacaceae

Perennial. The flowers are in a tight round head and with their conspicuous pink stamens they are like little pincushions. They are mauve to deep blue-purple, rarely pink or white, surrounded by green bracts (an involucre), at the end of along, erect, stiff stalk, with smaller, also solitary, shorter-stalked flower-heads rising from the axils of the stem leaves. These are opposite, narrow and sparsely toothed, becoming narrower near the top of the stem; the basal leaves are broader, stalked and sparsely hairy. The short root-stock ends abruptly, looking as if it had been bitten off, hence the name.

Meadows, pastures, damp woods, marshes. July — October.

2   Field Scabious   *Knautia arvensis*   Dipsacaceae

This is a larger plant, also perennial, and is much more showy as the outer florets have large spreading petals. The inner florets are spangled over with pink anthers. The flower-heads are lilac-blue, slightly more pinkish in the centre, and rather flat, solitary on long leafless stalks, and, like the Devil's-bit Scabious, often in threes, the middle one having the longest stalk. The narrow stem leaves are in pairs, stalkless and may be slightly lobed. The basal leaves are larger, stalked, and pinnately lobed or deeply cut, variable.

   Both are gynodioecious plants, ie. there are female plants and hermaphrodite plants. The all-female flower-heads are usually smaller.

Dry grassy banks, fields, pastures, commonest in south Scotland. July — September.

1.

2.

PLATE 118

1   Bittersweet, Woody Nightshade   *Solanum dulcamara*   **Solanaceae**
A woody perennial which scrambles over other plants, especially in hedges. The pointed, oval leaves are alternate, sometimes entire, but often have two spreading lobes at the base. The flowers are in loose clusters and have five, pointed, arched-back, purple lobes, from which project the pointed columns of the joined anthers. The fruit is a poisonous oval berry, green at first and red when ripe.

Hedges, woods, waste ground and shingle beaches. June — September.

2   Clustered Bellflower   *Campanula glomerata*   **Campanulaceae**
Perennial. The bell-shaped flowers are stalkless and are clustered closely at the head of the erect downy stem, often with extra flowers further down. They are usually blue-purple but very considerably in depth of colour. The sepal lobes are pointed. The upper leaves clasp the stem and are oval and pointed. The basal leaves have long stalks and are oval, rounded at the base and usually slightly notched.

Grassy places, especially on calcareous dunes. North to Kincardine. May — September.

3   Large Bellflower   *Campanula latifolia*   **Campanulaceae**
A tall, erect perennial with bluntly angled stems. The leaves are long, pointed and toothed; those on the stems having no stalks. The large flowers are in a leafy raceme, and vary from pale blue-purple to white. The capsule is rounded and nodding.

Woods and hedge-banks. July — August.

4   Ivy-leaved Bellflower   *Wahlenbergia hederacea*   **Campanulaceae**
A delicate perennial with thread-like creeping stems which bear short-stalked alternate ivy-like leaves, pale green and palmately lobed. The pale, sky-blue, bell-shaped flowers with five short lobes are stalked and rise from the leaf axils.

Damp and peaty places in the south and west, extending to Argyll, but rare. July — August.

1.

2.

3.

4.

PLATE 119

1 Scottish Bluebell, Harebell *Campanula rotundifolia* **Campanulaceae**
Perennial. The delicate blue bells hang in a loose inflorescence on thread-like stalks from a long wiry stem. The upper stem leaves are narrow and grass-like but at the base there are a few round leaves which soon wither. The bells vary considerably in depth of colour, and white form is sometimes found. The plant becomes very dwarf on mountains.

Roadsides, banks, heaths and hills. July — September.

2 Wild Hyacinth, English Bluebell *Hyacinthoides non-scripta*
syn. *Endymion non-scriptu* **Liliaceae**
The narrow, bell-shaped, delicately scented flowers have recurved tips and a pair of bluish bracts behind each flower; they hang down at the end of a long, pale green, smooth stem. The anthers are cream coloured. The buds are erect but as the flowers open they hang down. The leaves are long and narrow, shiny and smooth, rising with the flower-stems from a rounded white bulb. The fruits are egg-shaped with black seeds.

The plants spread into close clumps, especially in the west where they grow in great abundance. April — June.

3 Spring Squill *Scilla verna* **Liliaceae**
A tiny bulbous plant with long narrow spreading leaves all from the root, which appear first, to be followed by the sky-blue flowers in a close head at the end of a short smooth stem. They are star-like with six petals and six prominent blue anthers; they have very short stalks and each has a bluish bract.

Found on grassy places by the sea, common on the west coast but rare on the east. April — June.

1.

2.

3.

PLATE 120

1   Butterwort   *Pinguicula vulgaris*   Lentibulariaceae
The leaves lie in a flat rosette like a starfish. They are bright yellow-green, oval and pointed with in-rolled edges. The upper surface is covered with sticky glands which entrap insects. The solitary flowers, standing up above the leaves on leafless stalks, are violet with a white patch on the throat. The lower lip is flat with deep spreading lobes which are longer than broad, and the spur is slender and tapering.

Wet heaths and among wet rocks.   May – July.

2   Pale Butterwort   *Pinguicula lusitanica*   Lentibulariaceae
The leaves are again in a rosette but they are yellow-olive with a purple tinge. The pale lilac flowers have a yellowish throat and the spur is blunt and curves downward.

Bogs and wet heaths, rather local, in the west and north.   June – October.

3   Water Lobelia   *Lobelia dortmanna*   Lobeliaceae
The long smooth stems, which are leafless except for a few small scales, rise well above the surface of the water. The fleshy submerged leaves are linear with blunt ends, and arise in rosettes from the rooting stolons. The stem carries a few-flowered raceme of stalked, pale lilac flowers, widely spaced and drooping. The long corolla tube divides into two lips; the upper is split to the base and has two short lobes which are turned back, the lower has three longer pointed lobes. The calyx is short with small sharply-pointed teeth.

It is perennial and grows plentifully in the shallow acid water of many Highland lochans, where the spreading rooting runners form a mat on the stony bed.   July – August.

4   Lamb's Lettuce, Corn Salad   *Valerianella locusta*   Valerianaceae
A slender low annual with rather brittle stems that fork repeatedly in two. The minute, pale mauve flowers, surrounded by bracts, are in a dense flat terminal head, and give rise to distinctive round corky fruits. The leaves are narrowly oblong, unstalked and in pairs.

Arable land, hedge-banks and dunes, usually on dry soils when it is more compact in growth.   More common in the south.   March – June.

1.

2.

3.

4.

PLATE 121

1   Blue Lettuce   *Lactuca tatarica*   Compositae

A tall perennial with conspicuous lilac-blue flowers in loose clusters at the head of the stems. The ray florets are broad, strap-shaped and notched at the tips, and the inner florets are sky-blue; there are narrow bracts at the base of the flower-stalks. The upper leaves are narrow, clasping the stem, and are much larger than those at the base. Not a native plant but locally, and increasingly, common.

Damp, grassy places and roadsides. May – August.

2   Sea Aster   *Aster tripolium*   Compositae

The flowers are in small clusters at the ends of leafy stems branching from a stout, hollow, ribbed main stem. The narrow ray florets are pale mauve, the inner disk florets bright yellow turning brown. The fleshy leaves are long, narrow, half-clasping the stem, those at the base oval and dark green; all are untoothed.

Salt marshes, but mostly confined to estuaries in Scotland. August – September.

1.

2.

PLATE 122

1   Sea Lavender   *Limonium vulgare*   **Plumbaginaceae**

Perennial. The smooth stem rises from a woody stock with a rosette of broadly lance-shaped and pinnate-veined leaves which have a tiny spine at the tip, and narrow gradually into a long slender stalk. The erect stiff flowering stem does not branch till well above the middle when the angled stalks of the flower-spikes spread into a flat-topped inflorescence. The small purple-blue flowers are set closely in two rows on the upper sides of the spikes, each cluster with green bracts.

Muddy salt-marshes, southern coasts north to Fife and Dumfries. July – August.

2   Sea Holly   *Eryngium maritimum*   **Umbelliferae**

A beautiful plant of the sea-shore with its silvery-grey leaves and clear powder-blue flower heads. It is intensely glaucous, with stiff smooth branching stems. The stem leaves clasp the stem, the basal leaves have long stalks, both have a network of prominent veins, and are spinous toothed with a thickened white margin. The flower heads, closely packed and looking rather like teasels, are a clear bright blue and are surrounded by a whorl of sharply spiny bracts. The fruits are oblong and are covered with hooked bristles. Hooker, in his *Flora*, remarks, 'The roots are well tasted, when candied, and they are considered stimulating and restorative, having been so employed in the days of Shakespeare'.

Sandy and shingly beaches, but only in the south and west to Barra. July – September.

1.

2.

PLATE 123

1   Lesser Periwinkle   *Vinca minor*   Apocynaceae

A trailing, evergreen plant with long stems that root at intervals, with the flower stalks rising erect from the leaf axils. The flowers are solitary, violet-blue, with five rather square-ended petals that join below into a tube, with a circular white ring at its mouth. The leaves, growing in pairs, are oval, pointed and shiny. It spreads rapidly into a dense carpet in woods and shady places.

Doubtfully native but widespread. March — June.

2   Columbine   *Aquilegia vulgaris*   Ranunculaceae

The well-known flowers, like a circle of doves, are composed of five sepals and five petals, all blue. They are stalked and are loosely grouped on the tall, leafy, branching stems. The long-stalked basal leaves are twice trifoliate, the secondary leaflets usually stalked and irregularly three-lobed. The frilly double form grown in old gardens were known by an older generation as 'Granny's Mutches' or 'Granny's Bonnets'.

A local perennial plant of woods and wet places, native in South Scotland though naturalised elsewhere. May — June.

PLATE 124

1   Rayless Mayweed,   *Matricaria discoidea*   **Compositae**
Pineappleweed   syn. *Chamomilla suaveolens*

Not a native plant but very common now, especially by bare roadsides, tracks and trampled gateways to fields and farms. The yellow-green hollow, cone-shaped heads are prominent at the ends of the branching erect stems, which have much-divided lacy leaves at intervals. The flower-heads have a 'cup' of blunt bracts with rounded, dry, yellowish margins.

June — July.

2   Ribwort Plantain,   *Plantago lanceolata*   **Plantaginaceae Carl Doddies, Sodgers**

The commonest of the plantains, distinguished by its very long narrow leaves which grow from ground level, and are tapering, with from three to five veins, prominent on the underside. The dark greenish-brown flower-head is at the end of the long, furrowed, bare stalk. The tiny flowers open from the lower end upwards, with the long creamy-white stamens hanging out, giving a feathery look. As they fade and the seeds form the head becomes brown, hard and rough. The name 'Carl Doddies' comes from the children's game where two stand opposite each other, each with a long- and tough-stemmed flower, with which they hit alternately, trying to behead their opponent's flower. I believe this dates from Jacobite times and the '45, Carl being for Charles and Doddie for George.

Waste ground and fields. June — August.

3   Great Plantain   *Plantago major*   **Plantaginaceae**

The leaves are large, oval, sometimes irregularly toothed, entire, distinctly veined, and they narrow abruptly into long stalks which rise from ground level. The flower heads are on bare stalks, a little longer than the leaves; they are long, slender and green with whitish stems and lilac anthers. The seeds become black and hard.

Farmyards, roadsides and cultivated ground, always in the open. May — September.

1.

2.

3.

P<small>LATE</small> 125

1   Buck's-horn Plantain   *Plantago coronopus*   **Plantaginaceae**

A low perennial. Usually hairy, with narrow leaves in a flat rosette, variable but usually pinnately cut into several narrow lobes, occasionally lobed again. The flower-spike is long and narrow, spreading out and curving up, the flowers brownish with yellow stamens; the bracts are long and give the spike its greenish appearance.

Sea-cliffs, dry sandy turf by the sea. May – July.

2   Hoary Plantain   *Plantago media*   **Plantaginaceae**

Perennial. The broad leaves are downy and greyish, five to nine-veined gradually narrowing into a very short stalk and forming a flat rosette. The flower-spike at the end of a downy stem is scented, the whitish flowers having lilac or white stamens with purple stalks (filaments). Unlike the other plantains which are wind-pollinated, this is pollinated by insects. It is the least common species in Scotland.

Calcareous grasslands. May – August.

3   Sea Plantain   *Plantago maritima*   **Plantaginaceae**

The leaves, rising from a woody base, are erect, linear, fleshy, with veins from three to five long, but very variable, a great range of forms varying in size, fleshiness, and leaf teeth being found, apparently related to exposure or grazing pressure. The flower-head is at the end of long, erect, unfurrowed stalk, the flowers brown with four pale yellow stamens, and the green calyx of each tiny flower gives the spike its green appearance.

Salt marshes, sea-side turf, mountains. June – August.

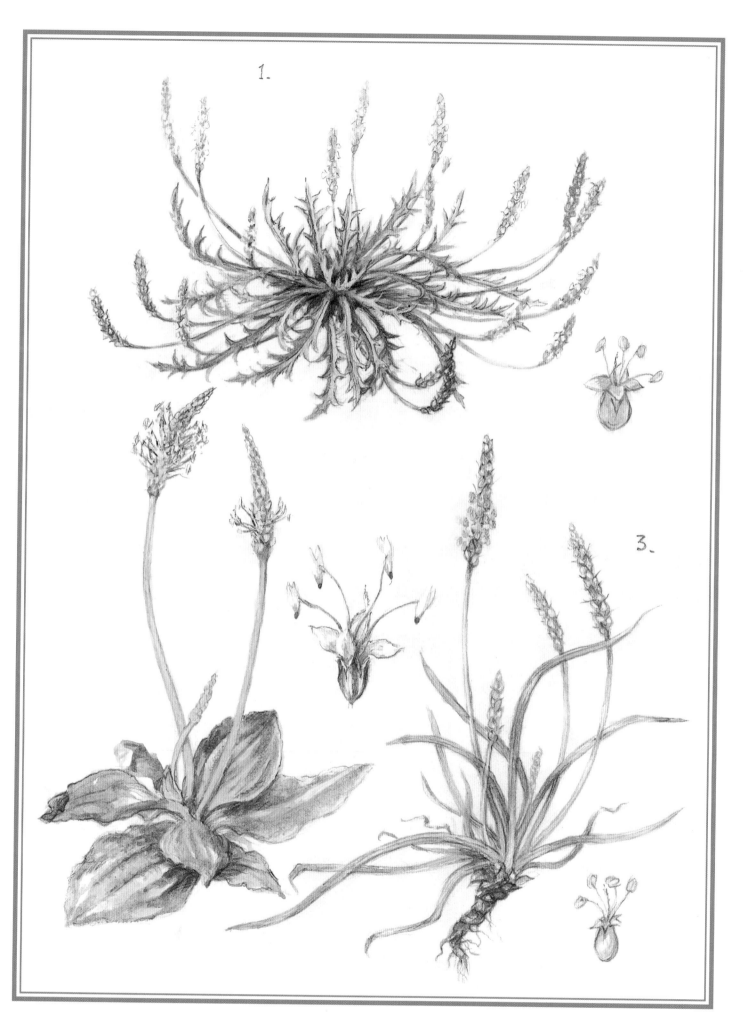

1.

3.

PLATE 126

1   Fiddle Dock   *Rumex pulcher*   Polygonaceae
A medium, spreading perennial, with long-stalked basal leaves waisted like a fiddle. Flowers in spaced out whorls on a long branching, leafy spike; they are drooping, yellow green, and the nut is 3-sided.

Waste ground. More in the south. June – August.

2   Curled Dock   *Rumex crispus*   Polygonaceae
Here the leaves are narrower with waved and strongly curled edges.   The inflorescence is less branched and the branches more erect. The perinath segments are broader, with the margins smooth or very minutely notched; usually all three have warts or tubercles. Very variable, and the commonest species.

Waste ground, roadsides, shingle beaches. June – October.

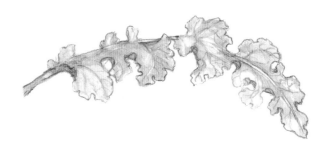

1.

2.

PLATE 127

1 Stinging Nettle *Urtica dioica* **Urticaceae**

Only too-well known. The rough, heart-shaped leaves are in opposite pairs, hairy and coarsely toothed, covered with stinging hairs that release an irritant juice when broken. The lower leaves are much longer than their stalks. The many clusters of minute green unisexual flowers are in drooping spikes hanging from the axils of the leaves, male and female on different plants. The stems are creeping and rooting at the nodes, with the tall erect stems, ridged or four-angled, rising in spring. The long yellow roots are branching, wide-spreading and very tough.

Abundant, hedgebanks, woods, grassy places, waste ground especially near buildings.
June — September.

2 Small Nettle *Urtica urens* **Urticaceae**

Annual. The oval leaves are in pairs, ridged, toothed sharply and deeply, the lower leaves shorter than their stalks, unlike those of the Stinging Nettle. The small green flowers are in much shorter spikes, again unisexual, but with both male and female on the same plant. The whole plant has a more compact, leafy appearance.

Waste ground, cultivated land, especially on light soils, rather local.
June — September.

3 Dog's Mercury *Mercurialis perennis* **Euphorbiaceae**

The erect, green, unbranched stem, ridged and slightly hairy, rises from a long creeping rhizome. The leaves are mostly together at the top of the stem; they are in opposite pairs, oval, pointed, with serrated edges, and have tiny triangular stipules at the base. The long-stalked flower-spikes rise from the leaf-axils, male and female on different plants. The male flowers, more conspicuous (illustrated), in longer spikes, have three green sepals and numerous stamens; the female flowers, also green and in long-stemmed spikes, produce the fruit, composed of two round, hairy, one-sided capsules joined together.

Woods, shady mountain rocks, especially on calcareous soil. March — April.

1.

2.

3.

PLATE 128

1 Cuckoo-pint, Lords-and-Ladies *Arum maculatum* **Araceae**
The leaves appear first; they are large and shiny, arrow-shaped, sometimes with dark purple spots. The long, pale green hood or spathe follows, enclosing the purple club-shaped spike or spadix, which has the rings of reduced male and female flowers below, hidden by the base of the spathe. The fruit appears after the spathe and leaves have withered, a close head of scarlet, fleshy, poisonous berries at the end of a short stem. The plant grows from a tuber, renewed each year.

Woods and shady hedgerows, common in the south but rare in the north. April — May.

2 Twayblade *Listera ovata* **Orchidaceae**
Easily recognised by the two large, unstalked, broad, ribbed leaves which curve round the stem a little above its base. The stem is tall and pale green with two tiny, triangular, bract-like leaves. It ends in a long spike of curious yellow-green flowers, the sepals and petals partly hooded, and the long lip hangs down divided into two deeply forked segments. There is no spur.

Moist, base-rich woods and pastures, dunes. June — July.

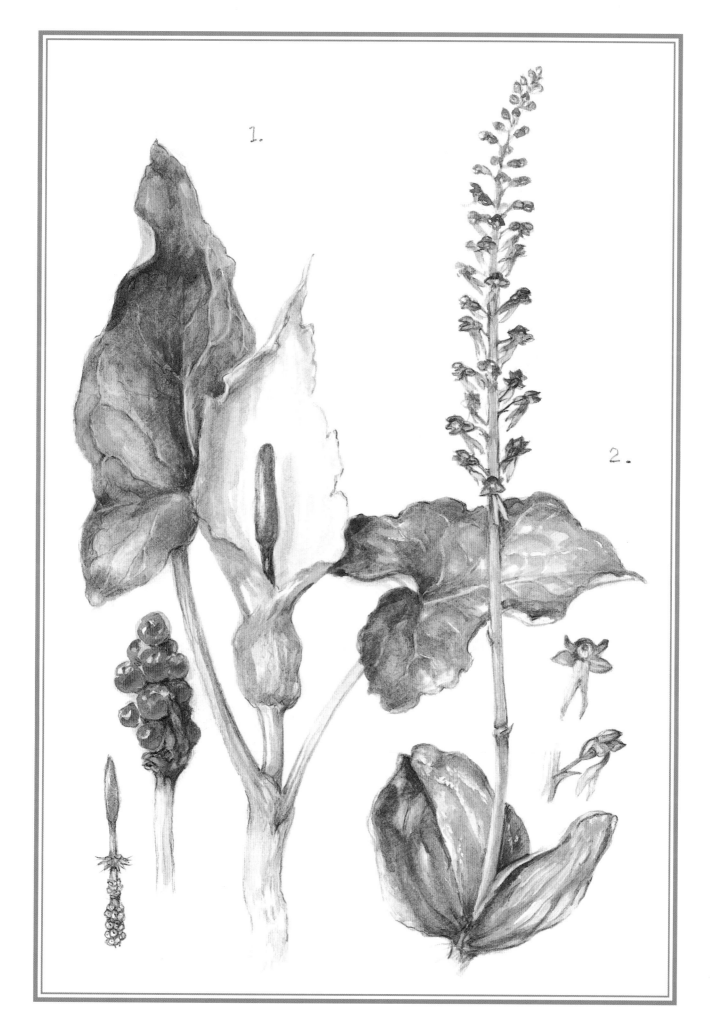

1.

2.

PLATE 129

1 Frog Orchid *Coeloglossum viride* Orchidaceae

The lower leaves are broadly lanceolate and the upper leaves are smaller, narrower, and clasp the stem which is short and often reddish above. The flower-spike is lax-flowered, with green bracts, the lowest about as long as the flowers. These are greenish and inconspicuous, with the upper segments forming a brownish hood which partly conceals the inner green segments. The pale, strap-shaped lip hangs down vertically with its tip divided into three small lobes. The spur is very small, blunt and translucent greenish-white.

Perennial. Grassy hillsides, mountain rock ledges, dunes. June – August.

2 Herb Paris *Paris quadrifolia* Trilliaceae

Perennial. The erect hairless stem is topped by a whorl of four (sometimes three or five) broadly oval, three to five-veined, pointed leaves. The solitary, long-stalked, star-like flower rises from the centre. It consists of four lance-shaped sepals, four awl-shaped green petals, eight long narrow prominent stamens, and a rounded purple ovary. The fruit is a black berry.

Damp woods, on calcareous soils, mainly in the east. Absent from west mainland Scotland north of Lanark. May – August.

3 Wall Pennywort, Navelwort *Umbilicus rupestris* Crassulaceae

An erect glabrous perennial. The fleshy, bright green leaves rise mostly from the base on long stalks and are circular, with rounded teeth and depressed at the centre at the junction with the stalk. The stem leaves are few, becoming smaller upwards with shorter stalks. The inflorescence is a long spike of many drooping, short-stalked, greenish-white flowers with bell-shaped, five-toothed corollas, and small linear bracts.

Crevices of rocks and walls, especially on acid substrates. West coasts north to Argyll and mid Inner Hebrides. June – August.

4 Marsh Pennywort *Hydrocotyle vulgaris* Hydrocotylaceae

A low perennial, slender, creeping, sometimes floating plant, which roots at the nodes. The circular leaves, with shallow rounded lobes, resemble those of the Wall Pennywort and are held erect of long smooth thin stalks attached to the leaf centre. The pinkish-green flowers are small and difficult to see, hidden under the leaves in tiny umbels on a short stem.

Bogs, fens and marshes. June – August.

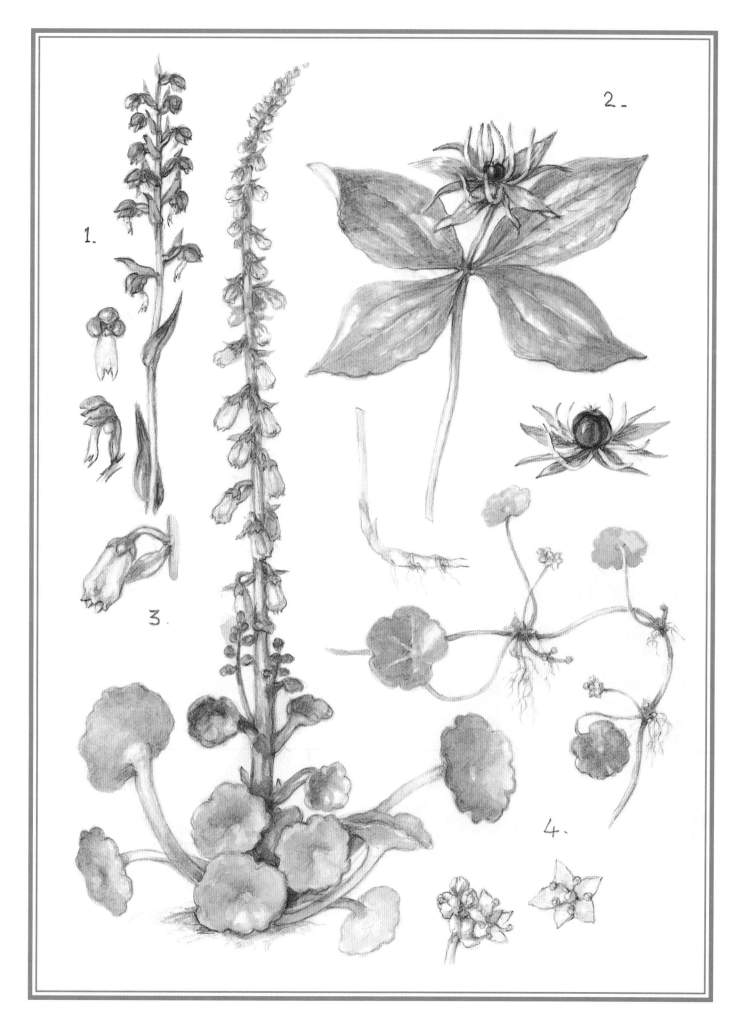

1.

2.

3.

4.

PLATE 130

1   Dyer's Rocket, Weld   *Reseda luteola*   Resedaceae

Biennial, with deep taproot. The tall stem is stiff, ribbed and hollow, with a few erect branches. The leaves are entire, narrow and oblong, they have undulating margins and are stalkless. The yellow-green flowers are in a long spike-like inflorescence, on very short, ascending stalks. They have four sepals, and four to five petals, those at the back and sides divided into three lobes, while the front petals are entire. The numerous stamens are curved downwards. The capsule is divided into three lobes.

A plant of disturbed ground, arable land, but rare and local in the north. June – August.

2   Salad Burnet   *Sanguisorba minor*   Rosaceae

Perennial. The branching stem rises from a rosette of long pinnate leaves with rounded sharply toothed leaflets which increase in size upwards. They smell of cucumber when crushed, and can be used in a salad. The stem leaves are shorter, with fewer leaflets, which are more oblong and have small leaf-like stipules at the base. The long-stalked green flowers are in a rounded head, with four sepals and no petals; the lower ones are male with many long stamens, the upper female with two red feathery stigmas, the central are hermaphrodite. The fruit is rounded, cup-shaped, four-angled and ridged.

On calcareous grassland, very local in Scotland but as far north as Dumbarton and Angus. May – August.

3   Moschatel, Townhall Clock   *Adoxa moschatellina*   Adoxaceae

A small, glabrous perennial with creeping, scaly rhizome. The leaves from the stem-base are long-stemmed and twice trifoliate, with rounded lobes tipped with a tiny spine. The two small leaves on the flower-stem are stalked, opposite and trifoliate. In the solitary, long-stalked close head of five, pale yellow-green flowers, one faces upwards with four lobes and eight stamens, while the other four, each with five lobes and ten stamens, face outwards at right angles – the townhall clock! The fruit is a green berry.

Woods, hedge-banks and mountain rocks, rather local. April – May.

Plate 131

1   Alpine Lady's Mantle   *Alchemilla alpina*   Rosaceae

This is perennial and has a rather woody stock which branches and is creeping. The leaves are mostly basal, stalked, with brown stipules, and are divided almost, sometimes entirely, to the base into from five to seven oval segments which are sharply toothed at the extreme tips. They are dark glossy green above and densely silky and silver beneath. The stem leaves are few, small, and have short stalks. The flowers are tiny, yellow green and in close clusters. Plants vary in size from very dwarf on high screes and mountain slopes to considerably larger in lower mountain grassland.

June — August.

2   Lady's Mantle   *Alchemilla vulgaris* agg.   Rosaceae

Perennial. Larger than the Alpine Lady's Mantle but very variable. The basal leaves are large, palmate and lobed, but never divided more than half way to the base. They are green on both sides and long-stalked. The stem leaves are much smaller palmately lobed and have whitish stipules. The flowers are in loose cluster, small, with yellow-green sepals, no petals and yellow stamens.

There are two clearly defined *Alchemilla* species, *A. alpina* and *A. conjuncta*, as well as the *A. vulgaris* aggregate which contains about ten micro-species.

Damp grassland, open woods. June — September.

3   Parsley Piert   *Aphanes arvensis*   Rosaceae

A small, inconspicuous annual with branches both ascending and decumbent. All along the stems are fan-shaped leaves cut into three segments which are further cut at the tips. The tiny green flowers, half enclosed in a cup formed by the fusion of the five to seven lobed stipules, are in clusters opposite the leaves.

Arable land, gardens, bare places in grassland, mostly dry soils, in the south. April — October.

1.

2.

3.

PLATE 132

1   Common Orache   *Atriplex patula*   Chenopodiaceae
A much branched, usually mealy annual, with the branches spreading or procumbent. The lower leaves are broadly diamond-shaped with projecting lobes on each side narrowing into the stalk, the upper leaves narrow and entire. The very inconspicuous petalless flowers, in a greenish spike, are slightly reddish but the tiny bracts which surround them and the rapidly maturing fruits give the plant a green appearance.

Very common and variable. July — August.

2   Frosted Orache   *Atriplex laciniata*   Chenopodiaceae
An annual, the whole plant has a silvery appearance, the branches procumbent and sprawling. The stems are often reddish. The leaves are oval with a wavy, slightly toothed margin, rather thick, and mealy on both surfaces. The inflorescence is in the axil of the leaves, and the bracts when in fruit are broad, rather rounded and sometimes toothed on the upper edges.

Sandy and gravelly shores about high-tide mark. August — September.

3   Hastate Orache   *Atriplex prostrata*   Chenopodiaceae
Similar to *A. patula* but distinguished by its wide triangular lower leaves, its ascending branches and less mealy leaves, which are broadly triangular and stalked.

Near the sea in waste places, less commonly inland. August — September.

4   Sea Purslane   *Atriplex portulacoides*   syn. *Halimione portulacoides*   Chenopodiaceae
A low shrubby perennial plant, with a short creeping, rhizome, and narrow, smooth, untoothed, mealy leaves, the lower opposite and stalked, the upper narrower, alternate and unstalked. The small flowers are in a dense axillary spike.

Salt marshes, especially fringing edges of channels and pools. West to Ayr and Outer Hebrides. July — September.

1.

2.

4.

3.

Index

Index of Botanical Names with Plate Numbers. Page Numbers follow (in brackets).
★not illustrated

Index of Common Names with
Plate Numbers. Page Numbers follow (in brackets).

★not illustrated